RAMS

04/02

ARBY	BARH	HIST
	11/99	8/96
MTRD	CTMOD	CAVL
3/95		
BASS	COMB	COTT
MELB	SWAV	W...

TANKS AND TRENCHES

TANKS AND TRENCHES

FIRST HAND ACCOUNTS OF TANK WARFARE IN THE FIRST WORLD WAR

Edited by David Fletcher

ALAN SUTTON PUBLISHING LIMITED

First published in the United Kingdom in 1994
Alan Sutton Publishing Limited
Phoenix Mill · Far Thrupp · Stroud · Gloucestershire

First published in the United States of America in 1994
Alan Sutton Publishing Inc
83 Washington Street · Dover · NH03820

Copyright © The Tank Museum, 1994

All rights reserved. No part of this publication may be reproduced, stored in a retrieval system, or transmitted, in any form or by any means, electronic, mechanical, photocopying, recording or otherwise, without the prior permission of the publishers and copyright holder.

British Library Cataloguing-in-Publication Data

A catalogue record for this book is available from the British Library

ISBN 0-7509-0346-5

Library of Congress Cataloging-in-Publication Data applied for

Typeset in 11/13 Bembo.
Typesetting and origination by
Alan Sutton Publishing Limited.
Printed in Great Britain by
Butler and Tanner, Frome, Somerset.

Contents

Introduction — vii

Chapter One
Flers — 1

Chapter Two
Arras — 21

Chapter Three
Ypres — 42

Chapter Four
Cambrai — 70

Chapter Five
Villers-Bretonneux — 95

Chapter Six
Hamel — 117

Chapter Seven
Amiens — 137

Chapter Eight
The Hindenburg Line — 172

Chapter Nine
Victory — 200

Introduction

In the *Tank Corps Journal* for March 1920, then just approaching its first anniversary, the editor made a specific appeal for contributions. 'This, then is what we want from you, a record of what you have seen and done, each one of you . . . Arras and Amiens, Flers and Festubert, your part in these was history and literature. And we want, not only the mud and smoke of it all, but accounts of the little amenities that made life endurable. . . . '. Judging from subsequent issues it was not the most successful of appeals, and when one thins it down to 'the mud and smoke of it all' there is not a great deal to choose from. But there is some, and what there is, is good. A year later the *Journal* began a new series entitled 'Tank Actions for the Month' which ran, off and on, until the June issue (of the now *Royal Tank Corps Journal*) of 1924, by which time the feature was beginning to suffer from rampant repetition. Selected items from both of these series provide the main element of this book and they represent what might be called a lost archive of superb, first-hand material, since it seems safe to say that most of it has remained almost forgotten for the best part of seventy years. To these the present editor has added other items from the Tank Museum library in the form of unpublished reminiscences, letters and official documents from the period.

All of these items have two specific merits. In the first place they are authentic, contemporary accounts, untouched by revisionist historians; in the second they were written by the tank men themselves, for their peers. Partisan they may well be, but they must have had the ring of truth or their readers would have spurned them. In what follows we have actions described by the men who were there, only a short time after the event, and they bring to light details that later historians have overlooked. One can get no better idea of what it must have been like to fight in a tank on the Western Front.

Naturally, this close to the action, one does not get much idea of the wider picture and, since the original readers shared the same experiences, little is said of the technical details of the tanks. In order to fill these gaps each chapter contains brief details of the kind of tank involved, while below an attempt is made to summarize the various actions.

The book is divided into nine chapters which endeavour to reflect specific periods in Tank Corps history. 'Flers' covers the original action on 15 September 1916 and some of the smaller attacks that followed. Naturally it was a period of innovation. The tanks, and most of the men in them, were quite new to war and their impressions clearly reflect this. Inexperience and unreliability combine to produce very indifferent results and it is evident that the new invention was not entirely welcomed by its own side. 'Arras' does little to improve things. Attacks are mounted in atrocious conditions with unsuitable machines and predictable results. Early enthusiasm starts to evaporate and the Australians, in particular, are alienated. 'Ypres' contrives to make things even worse. Pressure from other quarters sends the tanks into action over a sea of mud that will not support their weight, against enemy strongpoints which seem to be immune to their guns. There are one or two highlights but in general the results are dismal. Official support dwindles and the accounts have a strange, nightmare quality that reflects the almost unbelievable conditions.

With 'Cambrai' comes justification - for a while. Despite obvious weariness engendered by the long, wet summer there is clear exhilaration. Any risk, any effort seems worthwhile, even if it does all prove pointless in the end. 'Villers-Bretonneux' is a sharp riposte as the enemy takes the initiative. Again one detects a strong sense of unreality, with the world turned upside down, but there are brief successes and, overall, an impression of dogged resistance. 'Hamel' and its associated actions restores the advantage to the tanks. There is a new sense of power and professional confidence which wins the Corps new friends. 'Amiens' marks the high point. Tanks in large numbers sweep all before them and overpower the opposition. The Tank Corps comes of age and, for a while, seems to dominate all the other arms. The battle for the Hindenburg Line has been chosen to represent a series of actions which, while rounding off the success of Amiens, virtually destroys the Tank Corps by pitting decreasing numbers of tanks against strong enemy positions. However, the pressure is maintained while events in Germany sap the resolve of the defenders. 'Victory' has been chosen for the final chapter title since no particular name for a battle stands out. A new, more mobile, style of warfare is revealed in which Whippet tanks and armoured cars prove their worth. Again, however, the whole scene has an uncertain feel to it because the front-line troops have little idea where they are or what is going on. There is an impression of lost control on both sides which is only resolved by the fighting men themselves.

Whether any of the original contributions could really be described as literature is another matter. The present editor has weeded out some ponderous or irrelevant passages and matters such as the presentation of dates have been standardized, but in order to preserve a sense of period much of the original

INTRODUCTION

terminology has been retained. Thus, except in the case of the 17th Battalion, 'car' means a tank, as does 'bus' or even 'Willie'. Ranks have often been abbreviated and, except in rare circumstances, personal initials, honours and awards have been suppressed to save space and improve the flow of text.

The aerial photographs have been chosen from a relatively limited collection held by the Tank Museum, merely to illustrate the general topography and conditions in a region and not necessarily to show the precise site or date of an action. In each instance they have been reproduced twice: in a reduced size to link with the narrative, followed overleaf by an enlarged reproduction across two pages to allow a more detailed examination. Terrestrial photographs, wherever possible, do illustrate the action in question or at least something relevant to it. Anyone wishing to know more of the invention and development of tanks in the First World War is directed to the editor's book on the subject, at the time of writing the only such title in print.*

---

* *Landships; British Tanks in the First World War*, David Fletcher (HMSO, 1984)

CHAPTER ONE

Flers

The battle known as Flers-Courcelette was one of the last, wavering efforts to break the German line on the Somme in 1916. However, it is better known as the first battle in which tanks were employed. Just thirty-six machines of C and D Companies, Heavy Section, Machine Gun Corps arrived on the start line, early on the morning of 15 September, for their baptism of fire. In reality it was little more than a rehearsal for what was to come. Novice crews, many seeing the gruesome battlefield and coming under fire for the first time in their lives, fought harder to keep their machines running than they did to destroy the enemy. The fear they generated among those German troops that met them in battle was matched by the apathy, and even downright hostility, of those they were trying to help, and it is not surprising that their achievements were marginalized by the unimaginative.

The tanks they used were the original Mark I type, produced as males with 57 mm guns, and females with Vickers water-cooled machine guns. Powered by a 105 hp Daimler engine, the first tanks were slow and unreliable, while the driving technique, employing three separate gearboxes, required accurate teamwork in appalling conditions from four of the eight-man crew just to turn left or right. In these first battles the tanks were equipped with special tail wheels which acted as a counterbalance and steering aid, but they proved useless and were soon discarded. Another feature abandoned at an early stage was the wood and wire roof, intended to deflect grenades, which was fitted to some C Company tanks.

HBMGC BATTLE OF THE SOMME

On 1 July 1916 the Battle of the Somme opened with a successful advance on the British right between Maricourt and Orvillers, and a check on the British left between Orvillers and Gommecourt. From that day on, to the commencement of the Battle of the Ancre in November, no further attempt was made to push forward the British left, all available troops being required to maintain the forward movement of the right flank. The ground which separates the rivers Somme and Ancre is split into valleys by pronounced ridges, most of which form natural lines of defence for an enemy and could, in 1916, only be stormed after having been subjected to a heavy artillery bombardment. The ground had consequently become severely crumped in places, but as the weather up to 15 September had been fine and dry it offered no insuperable difficulty to the movement of tanks, which were allotted to the Fourth and Reserve Armies as follows:

Fourth Army, XIV Corps - C Company less one section, 17 tanks
Fourth Army, XV Corps - D Company less one section, 17 tanks
Fourth Army, III Corps - one section D Company, 8 tanks
Reserve Army - one section C Company, 7 tanks
GHQ Reserve - 10 tanks (all mechanically unfit)

On 11 September operation orders were received from Fourth Army and on the 13th a conference was held, which Lt Col. Bradley attended. During the 14th A Company arrived at Yvrench and at 4.30 p.m. on that day the headquarters of C Company moved to the Briquetterie near Trones Wood and the headquarters of D Company to Green Dump.

C Company tanks, a male and three females, preparing for battle. Petrol and grease cans are scattered around and the crews are attending to their charges. The grenade-proof wood-and-wire roof was characteristic of C Company but it was soon discarded.

The frontage of the Fourth Army attack extended between the Combles ravine and Martinpuich, the intention being to break through the enemy's defensive system and occupy Morval Les Boeufs, Gueudecourt and Flers. Simultaneous with this attack, the Reserve Army was to attack on the left of III Corps and the French on the right of XIV Corps. The attack was to be pushed with the utmost vigour and was to be followed by the advance of the Cavalry Corps, which was to seize the high ground about Rocquigny, Villers, Auflos, Reincourt, Les Bapaume and Bapaume.

The general idea governing tank movements on this, the first occasion of their use, was that they should be employed in subsections of two or three machines against strongpoints. Considerable apprehension existed as to the likelihood, on the one hand, of tanks prematurely drawing the enemy's fire, and on the other of their reaching their objective too late to be of assistance to the infantry. It was finally decided that they should start in sufficient time to reach the first objective five minutes before the infantry got there, and thus risk drawing hostile fire. Artillery barrages, stationary and creeping, were to be brought down at zero

The male tank C19 *Clan Leslie* moving up Chimpanzee valley with infantry for the first tank battle. The sponson door is open to let in as much air as possible. The steering tail wheels, typical of the Mark I, proved more trouble than they were worth, except for carrying stores, and they were later abandoned.

A Mark I female of C Company moving up to the front line. The driver's and commander's flaps are open to improve the view.

leaving lanes through which the tanks were to advance free from fire. The tanks moved up from their positions of assembly to their starting points during the night of 14/15 September. Of the forty-nine machines allotted for the attack, thirty-two reached their starting points in time for the battle, the remainder failing to arrive through becoming ditched on the way or breaking down with mechanical trouble.

The tanks working with the Reserve Army and the III and XIV Corps were not a great success; the operations of those with XV Corps in the centre were as follows. The tanks allotted to this Corps assembled on the night of 13/14 September at Green Dump, where the machines were tuned up for battle and where stores of petrol and oil had been collected. On the following night they moved up to their starting points around Delville Wood. Every tank was given the route it had to follow and the time it was to leave the starting point; this was in most cases about half an hour before zero (dawn) and was arranged so that the tanks would reach the German trenches a few minutes ahead of their own infantry. Briefly the orders were for eight tanks to advance on the west of Flers and six on the east of that village, their destination being Gueudecourt and the sunken road to the west of it. The tanks were to attack all strongpoints on their routes and to assist at any points where the infantry was held up.

Of the seventeen tanks which moved off, twelve reached their starting points; eleven of them crossed the German trenches and did useful work. One in particular gave great assistance to the attacking infantry when they were held up in front of the Flers line by wire and machine gun fire. The tank commander placed his tank astride the trench and enfiladed it. The tank then travelled along behind the trench and three hundred Germans surrendered and were taken prisoner. Another tank entered Gueudecourt and attacked a German battery, destroying one 77 mm field gun with its 6 pdrs. The tank was then hit by a shell and caught fire; only two of its crew got back to their lines.

The attack on 15 September, from the point of view of a tank operation, was not a great success. Of the forty-nine tanks employed only thirty-two reached their starting points; nine pushed ahead of the infantry and caused considerable

An oblique view of the battlefield taken a week before the attack proves that the tank men were not exaggerating about the state of the ground. Roads, trenches and the stumps of trees can just be identified, but the village of Flers (top right) seems reasonably intact.

FLERS

loss to the enemy; and nine others, though they never caught up with the infantry, did good work in clearing up points where the enemy was still holding out. Of the remaining fourteen, nine broke down from mechanical trouble and five became ditched. The casualties among the tank personnel were insignificant. Of the machines, ten were hit in action and temporarily rendered useless, and seven were slightly damaged but not sufficiently to prevent them returning in safety.

LT HEAD, TANK D3, 15 SEPTEMBER 1916

We left Elveden in Norfolk, Lord Iveagh's estate, and went to Southampton to cross over on 13 August, and the tanks went to Avonmouth. We met again at a place called Yvrench (near Abbeville) where the tanks were camouflaged and sponsons put on their proper fighting place. We got them fully fit and ready for moving up. We made our way to Happy Valley where all troops were waiting to go over on the morning of 15 September. We were there three or four days waiting for the weather and moved off at dusk. Everyone wanted to move at the same time; infantry, limber wagons, tanks and everyone connected with the next morning's engagement. The engineers had the job of laying white tapes for the destination or kicking-off point for each tank. The engineers, not knowing the capabilities of the tanks, laid the easiest route they thought along the edge of trenches, which was a big mistake as a tank must really cross as near right angles as possible. So we found our own way to our kicking-off points and through the sunken road, the site of my destination was Delville Wood, it was laid over the top with trench mortar shells. We tried to pull them out of the way, not knowing if they had been detonated or not. Eventually the Germans sent over some tear gas shells, on came our masks, but you couldn't see a thing so we had to do without. It would have taken all night long moving these bombs so I had a conflab with the fellow following me and we decided to go over them. We tested the ground and realized it was soft so the bombs sank in very, very gently and that was that. At the very edge of the wood we had to turn at right angles and pass along the front of the wood and wait for dawn. The fellow following me unfortunately got in the wood too far and got his tracks suspended on the stump of a tree. The stumps were not more than four feet high with continuous shelling for weeks on end and we manoeuvred into such a position to tow him out, which we did just before dawn. Dawn, I think, that morning was at half past six and we made our way very slowly towards Flers. On the outskirts of Flers, unfortunately, the tank got hit and that was the end of me for that day. At Gueudecourt on 28 September I was unfortunately hit again and that was that.

Signed H.G. Head, MC

Few photographs exist of tanks actually on the battlefield and even this is not quite what it seems. The Mark I male of C Company appears to be abandoned and the infantry are not going in the same direction, but the scene must have been typical.

LT A.E. ARNOLD, D COMPANY, 15 SEPTEMBER 1916

We waited for 9 p.m. [on the 14th] when we started off, with the noise of our Daimler engines lost in the battle effects of a continuous bombardment. We all moved off together, and were to cross our front line in pairs of tanks at various points. We were scheduled to advance just before the infantry, zero hour being at 6 a.m.

From Green Dump, our route led through Delville Wood, which had been the scene of much bitter fighting, and was now nothing but a pattern of shell holes with a few stumps of shattered trees. My own starting point was beyond Delville Wood, on the left, and in the direction of High Wood, where C Company were operating.

It was only three miles or so from Green Dump to my particular spot in our front line and I have always been puzzled as to why it took nine hours – from 9 p.m. to 6 a.m. – to traverse that distance, for we seemed to be travelling the whole time and certainly made no deliberate stops. But it was a case of bottom

Posed for the camera, troops cheer the Mark I Female tank C6 as she moves along a remarkably clear road behind the lines.

gear all the time, and on good ground bottom gear only produced a speed of about 1,000 yards per hour. But it was necessary at times for one of the crew to get out and scout for a way round a particularly bad patch.

As the dawn began to show the ground up we were still far behind the front line and it seemed certain we could not get there by zero hour for the going was now simply one succession of shell craters. But the ground was dry and it was thrilling the way the tank would go down into a crater, stick her tracks into the opposite wall and then steadily climb out. The rate of progress was now desperately slow and I suppose the last thousand yards took two hours to cover. We were getting nearer to the front line and although the infantry were out of their trenches before we arrived we now made better time, for no-man's land had not been so heavily shelled and the going was better.

We were into the German counter-barrage. Not all the tanks that left Green Dump ever reached the front line; some developed mechanical trouble and others became ditched. As we crossed no-man's land the other tank of my pair was just in front and a little way to the right and getting along well now that the ground was better. Suddenly she was stopped and emitting clouds of smoke. I saw the crew - or some of them - tumble out of the back door. This was not encouraging.

It was now half light; we were getting along better and were amongst the infantry who were in turn advancing and sheltering in shell holes as our creeping barrage gradually lifted. The German shelling was severe and one felt comparatively safe inside the tank. The German front-line trenches had been shelled practically out of existence and I think the infantry met little opposition there. And *Dracula* reached the support line first. A row of German heads appeared above the parapet and looked - no doubt in some amazement - at what was approaching out of the murk of the bombardment. At point-blank range I drew a bead with my Hotchkiss and pressed the trigger. It did not fire! Again I fired, and again the same result. But those inquisitive Germans gained only a momentary respite for the tank was on top of the trench and there we paused whilst the Vickers guns raked the enemy to port and starboard. Then on we went again, myself furiously attempting to make the Hotchkiss fire. Fool! I thought, you must have got excited, done the wrong thing and jammed the gun. I dismounted the gun and discovered the trouble. A shell splinter had struck the exposed portion and dented the metal guard over the piston. I mounted the spare gun - and tried it to make sure that it was firing.

Meanwhile it was growing lighter and we were advancing in the direction of Flers. The bombardment had slackened right off. Opposition was slight and the

D17, Lt Hastie's famous *Dinnaken* which Lt Arnold saw heading for Flers, photographed after the action.

New Zealanders, who were here attacking, were advancing and taking prisoner any remaining Germans. We soon covered the mile or so to Flers and on my right I saw the tank proceeding up the road into Flers [D17, Hastie]. The New Zealanders immediately set about consolidating the position and took possession of a sunken road which leads out of the village to the north-east. I sent off a pigeon with a message notifying the situation to Corps HQ. It was now about 8 a.m.; things were quiet except for spasmodic shelling and it was a lovely morning. Not liking the look of the German observation balloons I withdrew *Dracula* behind the shelter of a belt of trees. There we made tea and had breakfast; filled up with petrol from the reserve which we carried in a box on the stern wheels. We went over with fire extinguishers to see if we could help another tank that was on fire, but it was raging furiously, the ammunition going off inside like squibs. I moved our position occasionally as, from the incidence of shelling, I felt sure we were visible to one of the German sausage balloons.

A bit later on an infantry commander sent me a message; 'Counter attack brewing, and could I do anything about it'? We emerged from our lair, crossed the sunken road and went out to the front. We were rewarded with the sight of long lines of Germans advancing in open formation and opened fire with our port side Vickers guns at 900 yards range. It was impossible to tell just what effect our fire took but it certainly checked the advance. *Dracula* cruised about for a while in front of the village and then came under what seemed to me to be direct fire from a field gun. A difficult matter to judge, but someone was making useful practice against us. One shell in particular seemed to miss us by inches. I had, in the meantime, collected a bullet through my knee whilst outside. It was now late afternoon and as our infantry had been reinforced I judged it was time to get back. We had taken aboard a badly wounded New Zealander, and putting the village with its trees between us and the immediate front we made tracks for the slight ridge that intervenes between Flers and Delville Wood. We must have been visible to an observation balloon for we were faithfully hunted back by shells. Then after a while we were apparently ignored and as it grew dark we lumbered over the rise and out of sight. We handed over our wounded New Zealander to a doctor and proceeded on a toilsome way back through Delville Wood to our headquarters at Green Dump.

LT B.L.Q. HENRIQUES, C COMPANY, 15 SEPTEMBER 1916

We moved off from our camp behind the lines at 5 p.m. on the 13th. We went in a long procession and progress was slow as corners take some time in manipulating. Troops rushed to the side of our route and stood, open-eyed; thousands swarmed round us and we seemed to cheer people up as we went. At about 8 p.m. we got onto the main road. We covered 1½ miles in eight hours. To add to the joy it was pouring with rain. The number of trees I broke, motor lorries I damaged and ammunition wagons I jammed was high. The traffic was jammed both ways for miles. We got off the main road at about 6.30 a.m. and reached the point of assembly. There was a hard day's work ahead and we started off at once, cleaning and greasing. All our orders were given us very clearly, but about 4 p.m. the orders were changed. The enemy were still holding a portion of trenches which it was thought they would have been driven out of and so three cars were now told to attack these trenches and then carry out the original scheme. At 7 p.m. we left our place of assembly, Archie [Holford-Walker], George [Macpherson] and I were detailed for the work and we started in procession in that order. After 100 yards George stopped with engine trouble. This delayed us half an hour. Then we went on for another hundred yards and he stopped again, this time for good. Thus Archie and I proceeded to carry on together. The further we advanced, the more difficult became the track. There was a guide in front with lights, showing the way, and we had to go awfully slowly, continually backing to get out of the way of guns, etc. Down one very steep incline something happened to Archie's car. He came back and reported that he was out of action, and that I was to go on alone.

The Germans were strongly holding that part of the line, however on we went, the path becoming more difficult at every yard. When we rose out of the valley into what at dawn would be in full sight of the enemy, our guide was to leave us and most of the way was marked out with tape. Before we reached the brow I got out, stopped the engine to allow it to cool down and examined things generally. Archie himself had walked up with us and to our horror we found that more than half of the petrol had been swallowed up. It was midnight and I was due to start at 3 a.m. Archie ran back and, by really fine work, succeeded in getting us about 16 gallons by 2.30 a.m. In the meantime I had walked up to our front line to have a look at the route. I came back rather doubtful. Then we waited. I got fresh orders to leave at four instead of three. Four arrived and we steamed ahead, squashing dead Germans as we went. We could not steer properly and I kept on losing the tape. At five I was about 500 yards behind the First Line. I again stopped as we were rather too early. There was to be a barrage of artillery fire through which a space was to be left for me to go. At 5.45 a.m. I reached another English trench but was not allowed to stop there for fear of drawing fire upon the infantry so I withdrew 20 yards and waited five minutes, but nothing happened and I decided to go forward.

As we approached the Germans they let fire at us with might and main. At first no damage was done and we retaliated, killing about 20. Then a smash against my flap at the front caused splinters to come in and the blood to pour down my face. Another minute and my driver got the same. Then our prism glass broke to pieces, then another smash, I think it must have been a bomb, right in my face. The next one wounded my driver so badly we had to stop. By this time I could see nothing at all, my prisms were all broken, and one periscope, while it was impossible to see through the other. On turning round I saw my gunners on the floor. I could not make out why. As the infantry were now approaching and as it was impossible to guide the car, and as I now discovered that the sides weren't bullet proof I decided that to save the car from being captured I had better withdraw.

How we got back I shall never understand, we dodged shells from the artillery. I fear that I did not achieve my object. This is to be accounted for by the facts:

    i   The artillery did not put up the barrage.
    ii   Breaking of all the prisms.
    iii The non-bullet-proof sponsons.
    iv The fact that one car was not enough to do what three were intended to do.

My driver, servant and self were all wounded. It was like in a rough sea made of shell holes, the way we got over the ground was marvellous; every minute I thought we were going to stick.

LT V. HUFFAM, D COMPANY, 16 SEPTEMBER 1916

Orders came in August and on the 15th D Company sailed for France with 30 tanks. From Havre we went to another secret camp, Yvrench, some distance behind the British front lines. C Company were also in France and after more training, more demonstrations (General Joffre this time), we left Yvrench for the Happy Valley, a mile or so from Delville Wood. Here we were equipped; D9, my tank, petrol, oil, half a cow, pigeons, signalling flags and also 33,000 rounds of .303 inch ammunition, all this to be loaded into belts ready for the four Vickers guns in addition to one Hotchkiss gun. Whilst loading that afternoon we had yet another visitor who, having got into D9 by a small door two feet square, bumped his head on the low steel roof, let fly some real oaths. On turning to see who it could be, having sworn in reply, I was a little taken aback to see the Prince of Wales. He was followed by Bill Huffam, his ADC. He sat on the engine platform whilst we loaded and our store of stories was improved. He only visited D9 and we felt one up on our comrades! That night, under cover of darkness, we moved up to Delville Wood to our starting point and ready for dawn, 15 September.

And with the dawn 26 tanks rolled into action. In crossing a disused support trench Lt Cort, in command of D14, crossed his first trench. Halfway across it started to dig in, the parapet collapsed until his flywheel jammed. I was following him and I manoeuvred up to cross the trench and come in front of him, but this time the weakened trench collapsed, and D9 and D14 were immobile. We climbed to the roof of our tanks and watched our other tanks go in, immediately behind a creeping barrage. It was a wonderful experience, a barrage of terrific intensity, the rising ground in front seemed to disappear. Jerry, dumbfounded at our fire power, only to see for the first time our tanks rolling towards him, rose from his trenches back to Flers, but even there he couldn't stop our tanks and the uplifted infantry had him out; the battle, which had previously cost tens of thousands of lives, was over.

That afternoon a Chinese labour battalion dug D9 and D14 out and we commanders were ordered to proceed that night to Flers as the second objective, Gueudecourt, was to be attacked. On 16 September four other tanks, D2, D4, D7 and D19, which had stuck on the 15th, were also ordered to Flers, each officer to report next morning to various regiments, briefed for the attack on this fortress, six tanks and 50,000 men to take part. At dawn I reported to an Australian colonel. My reception was rude. I was told to take my bloody stink box away out of it, they were being badly shelled. Then I met Cort, who confirmed what I'd been told, the attack was cancelled. We had little time to be

The shattered hulk of *Die Hard* and her consort photographed outside Flers village some time after the battle.

glad; our CO, Major Summers, came along and told us the attack had been called off, but those orders applied to the infantry and not to tanks, and that our four other tanks had again become ditched, and now it was two tanks, no infantry, no supporting barrage and less than a mile away Gueudecourt, known to be a strong position.

With a very sincere wish from Major Summers, on a lovely morning in September, D14 and D9 started up. As D9 entered Flers piles of dead British and Germans were in our path. Attempts to clear a passage had to be abandoned, shelling was too intense, and eventually we left Flers. D14 was leading on our right and appeared to be smothered in shells. Our own prismatic mirrors and periscopes were already useless. My driver, Archer, had been blinded by splinters. I called my Corporal, H. Sanders, to take his place. We were now getting too much attention from Jerry. We opened our armoured flap to see where we were – we were almost astride the enemy Flea Trench, our two starboard guns doing terrible execution of the bewildered Germans. On moving off we watched D14, it appeared to stop and immediately exploded. I went to the port side gunners to see why their guns were silent. They never fired again, both gunners were dead I believe, several bullets and small shells had penetrated our armour plate, we were all in bad shape when we were hit by a larger shell, there was an explosion, then fire, and I came round to find myself lying on top

Lt Enoch's tank, D7, stranded after the action on 16 September. Some of the crew are outside with the infantry, and two wear the special leather crash helmets.

of my corporal, his shins were sticking out in the air. I had already been issued with morphia tablets and I quietened him with these and bandaged him with first-aid dressings from the others of my crew. We were close in enemy lines, with my corporal in agony and all others damaged and shell shocked. Later that morning the infantry attacked and captured Flea Trench, which lay between us and our own men, and I sent two of my men to them to get help. Whether they ever got there I don't know, but eventually our men went back and now we were in no-man's land. Sanders was in a bad way. I'd given him perhaps too much morphia to quieten his cries, but I knew that I had to get him back, and to help him and myself I fastened my belt to his, and as I crawled from hole to hole he came with me. Some time later I was with a Guards regiment and I was told that they and the Durham Light Infantry had seen our plight, and had brought us in. Six months later I was allowed to visit a Kentish hospital and in the entrance was seated in a wheeled chair Corporal H. Sanders, with Matron, sisters and a special guard. Whilst in hospital in Oxford I received a visit from Mrs Cort, Cort's mother. He and his crew of D14 were posted as missing, believed killed, and I had to tell her that her son was truly missing.

Signed Lt V. Huffam

HBMGC 26 SEPTEMBER 1916

The next occasion on which tanks were used was during the attacks on 25/26 September, five being allotted to the Fourth Army and eight to the Reserve Army. Of these thirteen tanks, nine stuck in shell holes, two worked their way into Thiepval and, after rendering assistance to the infantry, met a similar fate, and one, working with XV Corps, carried out the first star turn in the history of tank tactics which, in the report of XV Corps, is described as follows:

> On 25 September the 64th Brigade, 21st Division, attack on Gird Trench was hung up and unable to make any progress. A footing had been obtained in Gird Trench which our troops held from there northwards. Between these points there remained approximately 1,500 yards of trench, very strongly held by Germans, well wired, the wire not having been cut. Arrangements were made for a tank (female) to move up from here for an attack next morning. The tank arrived at 6.30 a.m., followed by bombers. It started moving southeastwards along the Gird Trench, firing its machine guns. As the trench gradually fell into our hands, strongpoints were made in it by two companies of infantry which were following in the rear for that purpose. No difficulty was experienced. The enemy surrendered freely as the tank moved down the trench. They were unable to escape owing to our holding the trench at the

The male tank C3, having taken a direct hit on the commander's side of the cab, lies in a shell hole. There is evidence of a failed attempt to dig it out. Another tank can be seen in the distance.

southern end. By 8.30 a.m. the whole length of the trench had been cleared and the 15th Durham Light Infantry moved over the open and took over the captured trench. The infantry then advanced to their final objective when the tank rendered very valuable assistance. The tank finally ran short of petrol south-east of Gueudecourt. In the capture of the Gird Trench eight officers and 362 other ranks were made prisoners and a great many Germans were killed. Our casualties only amounted to five. Nearly 1,500 yards of trench were captured in less than an hour. What would have proved a very difficult operation, involving probably heavy losses, was taken with the greatest ease entirely owing to the assistance rendered by the tank.

LT H.W. HITCHCOCK, A COMPANY, TANK 544, 13 NOVEMBER 1916

At five minutes before zero hour the engine was started and at zero hour Car No. 544 advanced and was directed by Lt Hitchcock on its course till about 7 a.m. when it reached the German front line and was temporarily unable to

French troops and a British officer examine the female tank C24 as she lies on the battlefield with a broken track.

proceed as the tracks would not grip owing to the condition of the ground. This had already occurred once in no-man's land. Up till now none of our own troops had been seen and the car was surrounded by the enemy. About this time Lt Hitchcock was wounded in the head and gave orders to abandon the car, and then handed over command to Cpl Taffs. Three men and Lt Hitchcock got out of the car; Lt Hitchcock was seen to fall at once, but no more was seen of two of the other three men who had evacuated the tank. The third man was pulled back into the tank after he had been wounded in the forearm and, as the enemy were shooting through the open door it was immediately closed. Fire was at once opened on the enemy who retired to cover and opened on the tank with machine guns and rifles. Cpl Taffs decided not to abandon the tank but decided, with the help of the driver, L/Cpl Bevan, who had been previously wounded about the face by splinters from his prism, to carry on and try to get the tank forward to its objective. They managed to extricate the tank by using the reverse and then drove forward as far as the German second line where the tank crushed into a dug-out and was hopelessly engulfed and lying at an angle of about 45 degrees, thereby causing the two guns on the lower side to be useless and the two guns on the upper side only capable of firing at a high angle. The tank was

A Company tank A13 *We're All In It* abandoned after having side-slipped into a trench.

now attacked by the Germans with machine guns and also bombed from the sides, front and underneath. At about 8 a.m., as none of our troops had yet been seen, probably owing to the thick mist which prevailed during the whole action, Cpl Taffs sent a message by a carrier pigeon asking for help. This message was received by II Corps who passed it on to the 118th Infantry Brigade who gave orders to the Black Watch to render all assistance possible. At about 9 a.m. the tank was relieved by a party of the Notts & Derby Regiment who were soon followed by the Black Watch. Cpl Taffs and the remainder of the crew left the tank when our line was established well in front of it and was safe from capture by the enemy.

The bodies of Lt Hitchcock and Gunner Miles were found and identified today. Gunner Stanley was seen being conveyed to hospital after the action. The guns have been removed from the tank by a salvage party and brought back to camp. Cpl Taffs and the men who remained in the tank with him undoubtedly did splendid work by remaining at their posts. I would specially bring to notice the names of Cpl Taffs and Lance Cpl Bevan (ASC driver).

Signed Major C.M. Tippets, commanding A Company, HSMGC, 14/11/16

CHAPTER TWO

Arras

The Battle of Arras, which began on Easter Monday, 9 April, marked the opening of the 1917 season on the Western Front. Much was hoped for it. Tanks were to help the infantry break into the new Hindenburg Line and clear a way for the cavalry to sweep through and roll up the German defences towards Cambrai. In the event, despite some early success, it was a disaster. Atrocious weather soaked the ground and disabled many tanks, while snow upset the preparations for one attack which resulted in serious losses among Australian troops at Bullecourt.

Since the new Mark IV tank was not delivered in time, the sixty machines that took part were Mark Is from the previous year, supplemented by some Mark II training tanks from Britain. The Mark II, while mechanically identical to the Mark I, had only been built for training purposes and was not properly armoured, which made it very vulnerable in action. All female machines were now equipped with the air-cooled Lewis gun which, although highly effective as an infantry weapon, did not function well in tanks and caused even more problems. By this time the four original companies had been redesignated battalions and brigaded in pairs in what was now known as the Heavy Branch, Machine Gun Corps.

D BATTALION, FEBRUARY AND MARCH 1917

It was unfortunate that 12 Company's parade ground for physical jerks and turning by numbers was at the top of that long hill to Agincourt. Day after day we toiled up that hill to do knee bends in biting winds which inevitably blew at the top. I've often wondered what Henry V and his satellites had to say about that hill in the 15th Century when they had to climb it complete with armour.

The dummy canvas tanks, soldier-propelled, which made their appearance in those days, were evidently produced to amuse the troops and were undoubtedly a success from the first. To see ten pairs of legs, representing either clutch or tracks, trying to negotiate a steep bank and slipping was quite one of the funniest sights imaginable. These tanks had a very short life and soon became part worn, and were put to other uses.

In the battalion itself, during the later stages of the stay at Blangy, two tanks per company were allotted, but they were in fairly hopeless condition. HMLS

Manhandling a dummy training tank through a French village behind the lines, clearly to the amazement of the locals.

Netta was a good example. She was sponsonless, would not go into three on one side and four on the other, would not go into reverse and one brake was completely worn out, but otherwise . . .

The battalion training ground consisted of two fields on either side of the Blangy–Humerveil road. In one it was necessary to dig the trenches essential for driving practice and in the other a rather steep natural bank was the chief item of amusement, especially to the numerous officers who stopped their engines trying to take it or who slithered down from the top, hopelessly out of control. The star day was when the company commanders took a tank out, but unfortunately the tankodrome on that day was strictly private.

C Battalion War History

At 8.15 p.m. on 8 April ten tanks of No. 8 Company attached to VII Corps and ten tanks of No. 9 Company attached to VI Corps, left their assembly

A line of tanks moving up to the front line for the Arras battle, with patches of snow still lingering on the ground.

position in the south-west part of the moat of the citadel at Arras for their starting points.

No. 9 Company led the way but on reaching the low-lying valley west of the Crinchon River, six tanks of this Company bellied badly before they could gain the railway embankment. This route had previously been carefully reconnoitred, and sleepers and brushwood laid over the softest places, but owing to the difficulty experienced in steering, and to ineffective brakes, it was found impossible to keep to the exact route. In any case the ground was most deceptive and, although comparatively hard in places, there was only a crust on top which concealed a treacherous morass below.

No. 8 Company and the remainder of No. 9 Company were fortunately stopped in time on the higher ground and managed to cross about 50 yards further to the west without mishap. Two of the bogged tanks were extricated by 2 a.m. and arrived at their starting points by zero hour. The remaining four tanks were all extricated during the early part of the morning but did not arrive in time to take part in the attack on the Blue Line.

The objective of No. 8 Company on the Blue Line was that formidable work known as The Harp which, owing to the width of the trenches and number and

The Mark II male tank *Lusitania* moving through the ruins of Arras to join the battle.

form of the traverses, was a most difficult proposition for tanks to tackle. It was afterwards found that the ground on the top of this plateau was very waterlogged and much blown to pieces with shellfire. In spite of these difficulties, half of this company succeeded in fighting their way as far as the string of The Harp before becoming bellied.

2nd Lt P. Saillard (C24) reached as far as the western edge of Noisy Work, where his tank received a direct hit, bellied, and was set on fire. Previous to this he had done valuable work in picking off enemy snipers and putting several machine guns out of action.

2nd Lt Toshack (C29) found infantry held up at Pot Trench and, accompanied by 2nd Lt Wareham's tank, proceeded to their assistance. The latter tank was put out of action by bombs but 2nd Lt Toshack kept the enemy's heads down with Lewis gun fire and took the trench.

2nd Lt Cameron (C39) found a gap in the attack where the infantry had lost touch. He engaged the enemy with Lewis gun fire until the infantry had time to come up and consolidate. During this time he routed an enemy machine gun crew and captured their gun. A little later the tank received a direct hit, killing one and wounding three of the crew. After attending to the

British officers examining the ground where Mark II male tank No. 777 *Charlie Chaplin* (C24) has stuck. The bolt-on extended track shoes were intended to prevent this.

wounded, Lt Cameron handed five of his Lewis guns and ammunition to the infantry.

2nd Lt Wareham (C23) had trouble in crossing the trenches but nevertheless arrived at The Harp twenty minutes before the infantry and did good work with Lewis gun fire until the infantry arrived. His tank was eventually put out of action by bombs being thrown below the tracks.

Of the ten tanks which started, seven bellied owing to the soft ground and three received direct hits from artillery fire.

The objectives of No. 9 Company extended from the northern end of The Harp (inclusive) to the River Scarpe. Four tanks were bogged before reaching the starting point and one tank became bellied at the starting point, so only five tanks saw action on this day.

2nd Lt Norman (C41) became bellied twice, owing to soft ground around Tilloy, and also had considerable trouble with his magneto. In spite of this he assisted the infantry in the capture of the village. He overtook them again about 300 yards from the Brown Line. Infantry in shell holes refused to follow the tank. It proceeded along and engaged the enemy on Brown Line with six pounder and Lewis gun fire. Two snipers were put out of action after considerable trouble and a Very light dump set on fire. The engine gave trouble again and the radiator was pierced by bullets. The tank remained out in the German lines till 3 a.m. on the 10th, when Lt Norman returned to Feuchy Chapel and filled up his tank with petrol at a refilling point near Maison Rouge. He attempted to go into action again on the morning of the 10th but, owing to holes in the radiator, was obliged to desist. The perseverance and pluck shown by this officer and crew was most marked.

2nd Lt William (C50) assisted the infantry in capturing the northern end of The Harp. The tank received a whizz-bang through the conning tower and bellied in front of Blue Line, and two guide rails of the right track were found broken. He managed to get his tank running after four hours but it bellied again near the Cambrai Road. He started running again after one and a half hours but eventually reached a point 400 yards beyond the Brown Line where the infantry were held up, but it was too dark to render assistance. He returned to the refilling point, and attacked the strongpoint next morning. While in pursuit of

A Mark II female which, from the attitude of those around her, also seems to be stuck, despite the array of track-extenders.

the retreating enemy, his tank was hit by a heavy shell, and the officer and two other ranks wounded and three other ranks killed.

2nd Lt Weber (C47), owing to his tank becoming bogged soon after leaving Citadel and having mechanical trouble at the starting point, did not catch up with the infantry until close to the Blue Line at Feuchy Redoubt. He knocked out an enemy machine gun with six pounder fire in a wood north of the railway. Infantry followed to Blue Line and the Germans surrendered. He then proceeded along the railway to Feuchy Redoubt and opened fire with the six pounder and Lewis gun. The enemy were observed evacuating their positions, some running away and some disappearing into dug-outs. He signalled the infantry to come on and assisted them in taking German prisoners hiding in the railway arch. Hastily abandoned guns were observed in Battery Valley. He then proceeded south towards Feuchy Chapel but was delayed en route through magneto trouble. On arrival at Brown Line he found the enemy holding a small redoubt. He received a signal from the infantry and turned in their direction. The Germans retired. He was then informed that two snipers were causing much trouble. He turned in the direction pointed out, when they came in with their hands up and were taken prisoner by an infantry officer.

Although his magneto was still giving trouble, and petrol almost exhausted, at the request of an infantry colonel who assured him his men would follow, he proceeded south along Brown Line still occupied by the enemy. He found four machine guns in action and eventually silenced two. The infantry did not follow up. The magneto then failed absolutely so Lt Weber kept his tank in action close to the trench and fired at every German head that showed. Being unable to move he decided to abandon the tank at 9.30 p.m., the crew leaving one by one and taking their Lewis guns with them. Unfortunately the tank received a direct hit next morning during a bombardment by allied artillery and was set on fire.

North of the Scarpe River, No. 7 Company went into action with eight tanks, all of which, despite having to cross an intricate trench system, reached their starting points without incident and started punctually at zero hour with the infantry.

The four tanks which started from Roclincourt, whose objective was the valley running south from the Bois de la Maison Blanche, had to cross ground of the worst possible description, and all became bellied near the Black Line in very soft ground where one received a direct hit from hostile artillery.

The four tanks of this company whose objectives were Laurent Blanchy and Athies were more successful, and three out of the four reached the Blue Line near the railway embankment north of the River Scarpe. Unfortunately these tanks were put out of action by direct hits.

2nd Lt Tarbet (C6) did excellent work with his tank and fought his way from the Black to the Blue Line, but on approaching the railway embankment,

Tank No. 599, a Mark II female, moving forward with infantry. Compare the Lewis guns in the sponson with the heavy Vickers guns, in their armoured jackets, on the Mark I female tanks in Chapter 1.

finding the country difficult to advance across, he got out of his tank to reconnoitre the ground in front and was shot dead by a sniper.

2nd Lt Innes (C42) of No. 9 Company assisted the infantry in clearing up the Brown Line near Feuchy Chapel. His tank did valuable work and kept the enemy's heads down until the infantry arrived on the scene and took them prisoner. The crankshaft of the engine broke and later the tank received a direct hit, all Lewis guns and articles of value having previously been saved by the crew.

After considerable difficulty, six tanks of this company were concentrated near Feuchy Chapel during the night of 10 April and were attached to 37th Division for the attack on Monchy le Preux. Orders were received for three of these tanks to start with the infantry and proceed round the northern edge of Monchy le Preux, and for three other tanks to start with infantry from Les Fosse Farm, to mask the machine guns known to be in the south-west corner of the village and then to proceed around the southern edge of the village. Zero hour was given as 5 a.m.

The company commander arrived at Feuchy Chapel at 4.30 a.m. and learnt that zero hour had been postponed till 6 a.m. as infantry were not in position.

A Mark II male tank crossing a shallow trench on its way forward. The piece of wood at the front is a torpedo spud attached to the track. It was used to help a tank unditch itself in muddy conditions.

Zero hour was afterwards postponed to 6.30 a.m. and then later to 7 a.m., the artillery bombardment to commence at 6.30 a.m. Of the six tanks that started, one bellied and its engine seized, and another broke its track; neither took part in the subsequent action.

2nd Lt Ambrose (C30) started from Le Fosse Farm soon after 5 a.m. On arrival at the crossroads at La Bergère the enemy appeared in force and bombed the tank, piercing the plating with armour-piercing bullets and wounding all the gunners. The tank was swung round in a circle towards Monchy and the enemy, under fire from the tank, took shelter in a sunken road. While swinging bombs exploded under the tracks, a few minutes later the tank received a direct hit from a shell which blew in one sponson. Lt Ambrose, however, got his Lewis gun into action from inside the tank and kept up brisk fire on the enemy who were again surrounding his tank. He afterwards managed to rejoin the infantry. He went into action with seven men, two of whom were wounded and four killed.

2nd Lt Toshack (C29) left Feuchy Chapel at 3 a.m. and started from Le Fosse Farm at 5 a.m. After arriving at La Bergère and turning north towards the

No. 599 again, astride a German trench with infantry in the background, probably stuck. The camouflaged female sponson, still mounting one Lewis gun, probably came off a Mark I tank. The plain brown hull of the Mark II was unarmoured, so at least the sponson would provide some protection.

village, the enemy was met in considerable force and engaged with Lewis gun fire. Three enemy guns, one from the Bois de Vert, one from a wood and one from The Factory, engaged the tank. It went on towards the village and was eventually hit and set on fire while stopping to change gear. Only three men, one of whom was wounded, escaped from the tank, and it is feared that Lt Toshack and the remainder of his crew perished.

Lt Salter (C21) reached the crossroads at La Bergère at 5.20 a.m. He worked his tank close to a trench on the south side of the road and cleared out the enemy with Lewis gun fire, afterwards informing the infantry that the trench was clear. He then started to work northwards towards the village. Soon after this the tank came under heavy shell fire and shell splinters came through the back door and radiator, killing the signaller and wounding the driver and four others of the crew. After dressing the wounded, Lt Salter, with the remaining two of his crew, went up to Monchy to try to get information but became cut off by the artillery barrage. He returned to the rallying point about two and a half hours later. There is no doubt that this tank was hit by its own artillery barrage.

Lt Salter's tank C21, a Mark II with Mark I female sponsons, struggling across the remains of a trench during the Arras battle.

2nd Lt Johnston (C26) started at 5 a.m. and moved to the north of Monchy. He encountered severe machine gun fire from the enemy in pits and put out several machine guns with six pounder and Lewis gun fire. He proceeded to the west of the village and then to the north and east. There was no artillery support and no infantry appeared until the village had been practically abandoned by the enemy. On arriving east of the village, he ran into his own barrage and the engine then seized, so he abandoned the tank and assisted the infantry to consolidate, supplying them with Lewis guns and several magazines of ammunition. He left the infantry at 2.30 p.m. and returned to the rallying point.

The services rendered by these four crews in the capture of Monchy le Preux were invaluable.

NO. 12 COMPANY, D BATTALION, 9 APRIL (EASTER MONDAY)

Zero was at 5.30 a.m. and from midnight onwards everyone had that depressed 'let's get it over' feeling which banished sleep. Nobody was pleased to hear the heavy rain that fell, as we knew the ground was bad enough without that to make it worse. There was only a little intermittent shelling going over – nothing coming back, and the silence at times was uncanny. At last only five minutes to go and all the engines were gently ticking over, much to the relief of the section commanders, Lts Robinson and Head.

Zero hour brought pandemonium, more especially in Hunland! The Canadians were over the top and the eight tanks of sections 9 and 10 some few hundred yards behind with the idea of catching them up for the advance to the second objective beyond the Lens–Arras road. A tank feels conspicuous on the top, but certainly gives a sense of protection from machine guns and splinters! Skirting Neuville St Vaast Cemetery No. 12 Company went hell for leather (at 3 m.p.h.) for the British front line.

But the company was fated not to catch up with the infantry. On passing Litchfield, Pulpit and Zivy Craters we reached Hunland and the shelled area, which the night's rain had turned into a sponge, quite unable to bear 30 tons or so. Before the Boche second line was reached every commander was outside picking a way for his tank, but even that method was of no use and half-way to the Lens road every single tank had bellied and remained so despite two or three hours' spade work by the crews. In those days there were no unditching beams and the spars and spuds with which the tanks were fitted were useless and only served to catch up and wind all loose wire around the tank. There was nothing to do but to stand by for orders, which Major Watson brought personally during the afternoon when the crews were withdrawn to camp. Luckily there was no stopping the Canadians that day and they took all their objectives.

Naturally the disappointment at not getting into action was very keen, but Mark IIs could not achieve the impossible. The casualties were small, about a dozen all told, including Lts Morgan and Preshous, and were mostly caused by shelling during the endeavours to unditch. The cars themselves were dug out in the following few days by means of large working parties with plenty of spades, wood, etc.

Meanwhile at Arras, No. 10 Company, in spite of running into a bog on the trek up to the starting point, had fortunately found better going and was carrying on a very successful attack round Telegraph Hill. Here, the tanks acting to a great extent as individual units, did heavy execution, some remaining in action till well on in the afternoon before withdrawing to refill for subsequent attacks, of which that on Neuville Vitasse on the 11th was particularly successful, large numbers of the enemy being rounded up during the eight hours or so that the tanks were in action. One tank was reported to be running round on its own for about three days, assisting the infantry here, there and everywhere. The casualties of No. 10 were considerably heavier than those of No. 12 and unfortunately Lt Rankin, attached to that unit, was killed.

An oblique view of the battlefield near Bullecourt, showing the vast trench system of the Hindenburg Line and the massive belts of wire – the darker strips, bottom left – which protected it.

While Nos 10 and 12 Companies of D Battalion had been in action up north, No. 11 Company, under Major Watson, had been moving up from Behagnies via Mory Copse for an attack on the Bullecourt–Noreuil line, in conjunction with the Australians, on 10 April. Unfortunately a heavy fall of snow on the night of the 9th upset calculations, making it impossible to be in position by the morning of the 10th, and at the last minute the attack had to be postponed for 24 hours. But by dawn of the 11th all arrangements had been satisfactorily completed.

At zero on 11 April three sections of four tanks, under Captains Wyatt, Field and Spears, each moved forward in front of the infantry to attack their objectives. This entailed moving over a wide, snow-covered no-man's land and the enemy was not slow to take advantage of the prominent targets which stood out so clearly against the snow. The two right-hand sections stood no chance against the direct fire of the field guns and practically every tank was knocked out by one or more direct hits and, as may be imagined, the casualties were tremendously heavy. The following infantry were thus left without support and

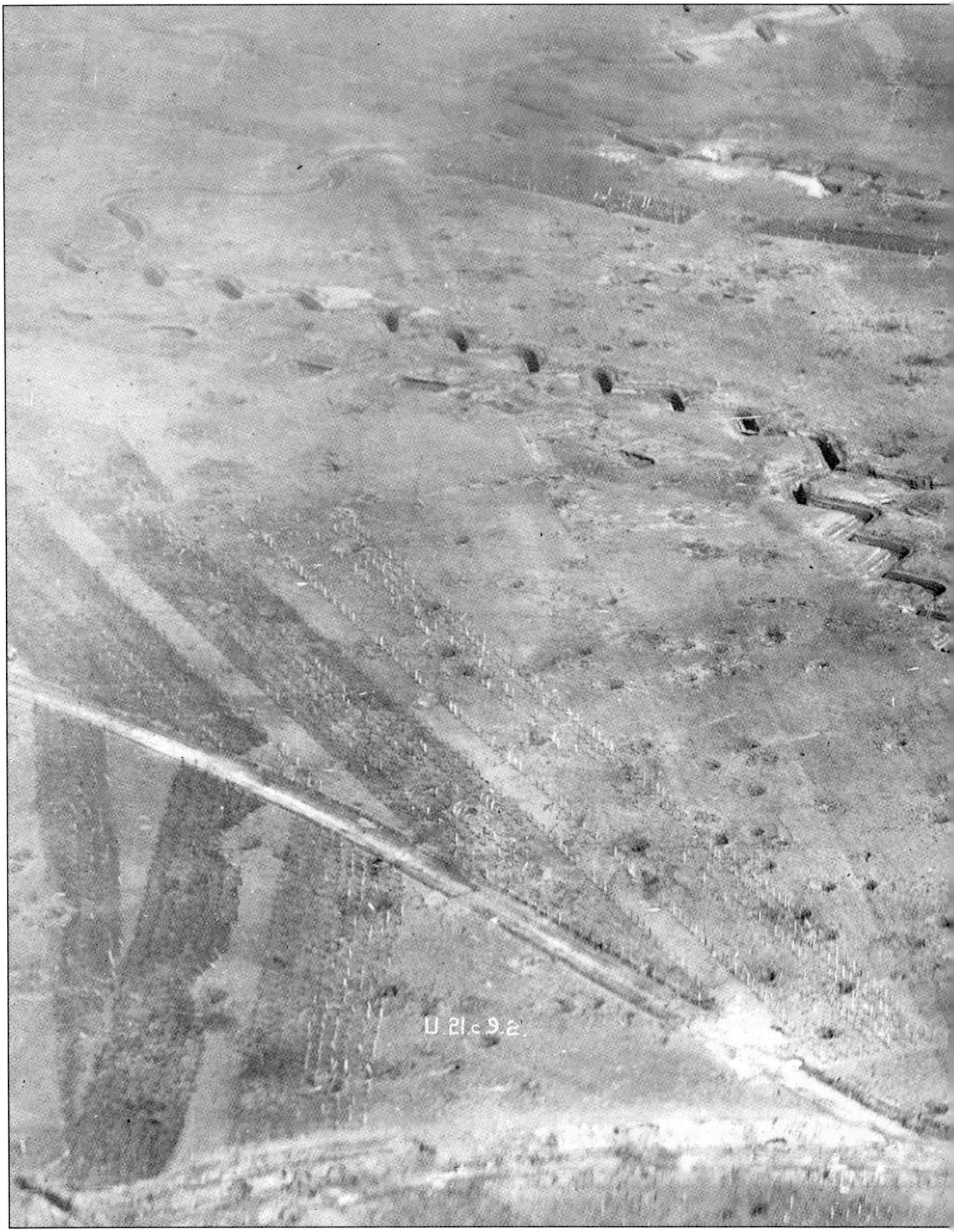
U.21.c 9.2.

S.W. Bullecourt

U.27.b.1.9.

means of getting through the wire and were able to make little progress against the heavily fortified Hindenburg Line.

The left section met with better success, although two of the four tanks were put out of action early on. The other two, under Lts Davies and Clarkson, pushed on as fast as possible to their objectives, followed by their supporting infantry, consisting of several hundred Australians. By magnificent fighting Riencourt and Hendecourt, some miles behind the original line, were taken. But without support on the flanks it was impossible to hold them and as a result the whole party was surrounded by a strong enemy counterattack and was unable to fight its way back. The section commander, Capt Swears, very bravely went forward on foot to discover the fate of his two tanks, but unfortunately was never seen again.

Not a single tank of the three sections survived the action. The survivors of the personnel were therefore withdrawn to camp at Behagnies.

At dusk on 1 May the ten tanks of No. 12 Company moved out for the trek of two miles to Mory Copse, the first stage of the journey to the line, and on. The second stage commenced on 2 May as soon as it was dark, under the guidance of the Company Reconnaissance Officer, or 'Contours' for short.

It was about 3½ miles to the starting point at the railway embankment at Ecoust St Mein, and to avoid all risk of detection the journey was carried out at minimum speed, with a barrage by the artillery and machine guns arranged to cover any noise between the hours of 8 p.m. and 12 midnight. The fact that the exhaust pipe was on top of the tank, and not at the back as in later tanks, also had to be taken into consideration and the column, silently and with no lights showing, duly arrived at the embankment at midnight. Engines were shut off to allow them to cool, and 9 and 10 Sections waited for zero.

The Hun shelled a good deal during the night and was evidently expecting something. All night the infantry of 62nd Division crowded past and over the embankment to deploy in no-man's land and at zero − 5 a.m., our engines were all ticking over.

At 3.45 a.m. on 3 May there was the usual 'Hell-let-loose' from our side and the answering rainbow of Very lights from the Boche trenches. Six tanks moved forward with the infantry, two operating north of Bullecourt, two frontally and two south. The remaining two were to follow 45 minutes later to go through and exploit. Further north near Croisilles three tanks of No. 11 Company under Capt Haig also participated in the attack.

The Germans were undoubtedly expecting us and the wide no-man's land was filled with gas. All six tanks reached the Boche front line. The two northern ones, both females, commanded by Lts Chick and Cooney, moved up and down, machine gunning heavily, but were unable to make substantial headway

A female tank, probably out of action, behind a British eighteen-pounder battery, with masses of cavalry in the background.

with machine guns only against the heavily fortified positions. The infantry, badly gassed, were unable to penetrate the 30 to 40 yards of wire in any numbers in support. Then the armour-piercing bullets began to take their count and both officers and a number of the crews were wounded. Of the two centre tanks, Lt Lawrie's was knocked out almost immediately by direct hits and Lt Westbrook worked up and down the line doing execution with his six pounders until he too was put out of action.

The southern tanks met with little better success. Lt McCoull was temporarily blinded by concentrated machine-gun fire on the front of the tank, and as far as is known drove into a trap consisting of a deep pit specially dug. Only one of the crew returned and he was unable to say definitely what had happened. The other tank commander, Lt Knight, suffered heavy casualties on account of armour-piercing bullets and was unable to carry on fighting. He returned to the starting point, picked up a fresh crew and again returned in broad daylight to Bullecourt, but after several hours in action had to withdraw as he was unsupported.

Meanwhile the remaining two tanks, under Lts Lambert and Smith, had moved up with a view to exploitation but found this impossible. On reaching the outskirts of the village they were subjected to concentrated machine-gun fire, and Lt Lambert and most of his crew were wounded, whilst in Lt Smith's tank an armour-piercing bullet exploded the cordite of a six pounder shell, setting the tank on fire internally. Evacuation became necessary and although the fire was eventually got in hand, casualties made it impossible to carry on.

The two reserve tanks of the Company under Lts Dobinson and Clark had moved up from Mory to Ecoust embankment, but as the attack had been well held Major Ward wisely decided that to send them in would be a waste of men and material.

The result of the attack was a tremendous disappointment to all as we had fondly imagined exploiting into the blue. The casualties among the men were heavy and of the tank commanders seven out of eight were wounded but two returned to duty after treatment at No. 45 Casualty Clearing Station. The following day was spent counting the number of holes in each tank caused by armour-piercing bullets, one tank having between 20 and 30. For this action three MCs, one DCM and about ten MMs were awarded to the company.

1ST TANK BRIGADE, 11 APRIL 1917

Eleven out of the 12 tanks started off at 4.30 a.m. in line at 80 yard intervals and about 800 yards from the German line. Four tanks attacked Bullecourt and two the Hindenburg Line to the north-west. Two of the former were knocked out in the village and two returned damaged – both those on the Hindenburg Line were knocked out by shell fire while waiting for the infantry. Three tanks advanced on Riencourt and Hendecourt. One of these was knocked out while the other two, operating with 200 Australian infantry, cleared Riencourt and then advanced on Hendecourt, clearing that village also. Of the two tanks operating against the Hindenburg Line to the eastwards, one was knocked out and the other returned safely.

In this operation tanks replaced the barrage, covering and opening the way for the infantry attack – and the tank operations were excellently and most gallantly carried out. The ground was covered in snow and gave the enemy artillery a great advantage as regards observation of the tanks.

27TH GERMAN DIVISION, 11 APRIL 1917

The machine guns at the fore end of the tanks open fire when within 500 to 100 yards of our lines. The guns of the male tanks can only fire to the front and to the side. Their arc of fire is considerable. On reaching or passing our trenches the majority of the tanks turn to the right or left, to assist the infantry in the mopping up of trenches. Odd tanks go ahead to enable the infantry to breach our lines.

Ordinary wire entanglements are easily overcome by the tanks. Where there are high, dense and broad entanglements, such as those in front of the Hindenburg Line, the wire is apt to get entangled with the tracks of the tanks. On 11 April one tank was hopelessly stuck in our wire entanglement. Deep trenches, even eight feet wide, seem to be a serious obstacle to tanks.

At long ranges by day, tanks will be engaged by all batteries that can deliver fire with observation and that are not occupied with other more important tasks. All kinds of batteries put tanks out of action on 11 April. Battery commanders must be permitted to act on their own initiative to the fullest possible extent. By night fire at short ranges only promises good results. The 11 April proved that rifle and machine-gun fire with armour-piercing ammunition can put the tanks out of action. Fire directed at the sides of the tanks is more effective than fire at the fore end. The greatest danger for the tanks is the ready inflammability of the petrol and oil tanks. Machine-gun fire is capable of igniting them. The garrison of the trench will take cover behind the traverses and will direct their fire at the

Two knocked-out British tanks, seen from behind a captured German gun position. Artillery, dug in and protected like this, would be invisible to a tank until it was too late.

hostile infantry following the tanks; firing on tanks with ordinary small arms ammunition is useless.

Anti-tank guns are indispensable; they are particularly useful for combatting tanks which have penetrated our lines and are within our front lines; however, the anti-tank guns are a source of danger to our own infantry. On 11 April seven tanks were put out of action by artillery, three being settled by anti-tank guns. The most effective weapons against tanks would be small trench guns served by the infantry, which should be kept in dug-outs up to the actual moment of coming into action when they deliver fire at point-blank range. These guns should be nearly as easy to handle as machine guns.

Trench mortars of all kinds are also suitable for anti-tank defence. On 11 April a light trench mortar put a tank out of action. The moral effect of tanks on the infantry is very great; it is somewhat minimized in this division by the successful repulse of the tank attack on 11 April. The actual effect of the tank guns and machine guns must not be underestimated; 124th Infantry Regiment suffered considerable losses from them on 11 April. The issue to the infantry of plenty of armour-piercing ammunition and trench guns would put into their hands weapons which could bring to an end all tank attacks.

BULLECOURT, 11 APRIL 1917

Like most others who heard the report that two tanks followed by infantry had penetrated to Hendecourt (far behind the Hindenburg trenches) the writer at first accepted it as accurate. He had closely watched the battle and had been under the impression (though he could not be sure) that one of the two tanks which he saw in motion was just beyond the Hindenburg Line, although nowhere near Hendecourt.

When, however, within the next week or two he visited the units which had taken part in it, and spent some evenings digging out the details of the fighting with the assistance of officers who had been in the thick of it, he found them, without exception, positive that only one tank had crossed the Hindenburg wire – and that after the troops; and that although this same tank subsequently crossed the first trench it did not reach the second, but returned to the first and broke down there.

A second reached the wire and was destroyed there; a third, late in the day, reached the south-east corner of Bullecourt and became immovable in a deep crater. All the evidence of eye witnesses agreed as to these three; but not one officer or man questioned had seen or heard of any tank passing the second trench. On the contrary all were positive that no tanks crossed it.

German troops examining a knocked-out Mark II male tank. Despite the advantages of this opportunity, the Germans seem to have been slow to appreciate the capabilities of tanks. Certainly this investigation seems to have been a lighthearted affair.

Subsequently the diary of the German Corps Commander, the history of the German division concerned, and the histories of all the three German regiments holding the line that day came to hand. They mention every tank the Germans saw that day. Not one had crossed the second trench, but one lost direction, wandered far to the right and eventually crossed, not the Hindenburg Line, but the front line of Balcony Trench around Queant, and was there put out of action by a machine gun and the crew killed.

                    Signed C.E.W. Bean, Official Australian Military Historian

CHAPTER THREE

Ypres

For the summer of 1917 Haig turned his attention to Flanders and mounted another major offensive. Even in good weather it was not an ideal region for tanks. The water table was high at the best of times but artillery had pulverized the ground and destroyed the drainage. Since it was a very wet summer, conditions all along the front were atrocious; the ground was a quagmire, almost impassable to men, never mind 28 ton tanks. In place of trenches the Germans used massive concrete blockhouses and gun pits which the British struggled through liquid mud to subdue. Conditions for the tanks were impossible yet they were continually committed to action and just as regularly bogged down, until their value as a weapon was being seriously questioned. It was for conditions like these that equipment such as the unditching beam was devised.

The Mark IV tank, which first saw action at this time, was the final production model of the Mark I type. It had the same engine and transmission but many features had been redesigned to improve performance, reliability and safety, including thicker armour and an external fuel tank. It was the most prolific British tank of the Great War, some 1,200 being built. The title Tank Corps was adopted in June 1917, and by August 1917 nine battalions were in France.

G BATTALION, 31 JULY 1917

At dusk on 30 July Capt Syme left Frascati in charge of a taping party. He laid tapes right up to the starting point at Bilge Trench and met the tanks at Hammonds Corner during their wait there. It was due to his careful preparation of the route that all tanks reached their starting point. Capt Syme made arrangements for a lamp to be in our front-line trench to guide the company over. Once over no-man's land he led his tanks on to their proper course and then followed them up on foot, rendering assistance when any became ditched.

I was with him in a shell hole taking cover from machine-gun fire near Juliet Farm, but he would not remain under cover and went off to the assistance of one of his tanks which was then catching us up. He appears to have been seen near St Julien still giving directions and was finally wounded in the leg. He was carried into one of our tanks (Lt Gardner) and brought to the dressing station.

Signed B.L. Henriques, Lt Reconnaissance Officer, XIX Company, No. 1 Section, G Battalion

TANK G1, 2/LT McCHLERY

Tank left Frascati Farm about 11.30 p.m. on 30 July and proceeded by taped route to jumping-off point at Bilge Trench. Zero was at 3.50 a.m. on 31 July. At 3.56 a.m. infantry advanced and I proceeded behind them, crossing no-man's land, Canadian Trench and Canadian Support in the dark without much difficulty. As it got lighter I found myself to the left of my proposed route and proceeded to my right to get on to it. At 4.30 a.m. another tank drew ahead of me and got ditched directly in front of me, and I had to draw to the right to avoid it, and in doing so got badly ditched at 4.50 a.m. in very marshy ground. My tank was almost up to the six pounder guns in mud. I got my crew out and the unditching gear fitted on and started digging the mud from in front of the sponsons. At this time the enemy started shelling his own front line, just behind us, and a machine-gun barrage also seemed to be passing over us. My tank seemed to be sinking further into the mud so I put out the white square showing myself out of action. About 6.20 a.m., after a severe struggle, my tank drew out on to a piece of firm ground. At 6.50 a.m. I proceeded on my route. The ground was very heavily shelled and I had to keep on first speed. I passed Oblong Farm and made for Canopus Trench. Just north-east of Oblong Farm my carburettor became choked and I had to stop from 8.00 a.m. to 8.20 a.m. to rectify it. During this stoppage I was heavily shelled. Got going again and was under heavy shell fire until I reached Canopus Trench. Found infantry consolidating in Canopus Trench and Falkenheyn Redoubt. Saw two tanks ditched north-east of Juliet Farm. Pushed on across Canopus towards Steenbeek. After crossing Canopus appeared to come under direct observation of shells from heavy guns, landing alternately a few yards in front and behind and making it very difficult to observe from the driver's seat. Ground one mass of shell holes. Engine started giving trouble. Exhaust red hot. Engine not pulling and back firing. Carburettor had to be kept raised by hand. Decided not to cross Steenbeek as infantry could be seen already across and advancing on Green Line. Pushed on to St Julien and arrived about 10.10 a.m. Infantry in possession of St Julien. Sent off pigeon message. Owing to engine trouble decided to return to rallying point. Again came under heavy shell fire. Reached rallying point at about 11.00 a.m. No other tanks of my section or section commander were to

Two Mark IV tanks. A camouflaged male stuck in a shell hole and a damaged female ahead of it, with dead or wounded soldiers.

be seen. As we were being heavily shelled still, decided to make for Company rallying point, but owing to weakness of engine had to choose best ground and go by round-about route towards Racecourse Farm. South-east of Racecourse Farm saw Major Fernie, asked for orders and was told to take cover behind some pollards near Kultur Farm. Tank G10 [2/Lt Jordan] rallied with me at this point. Camouflaged tank. One man wounded by shell splinter. Sent off pigeon message at 5.30 p.m.; ordered to withdraw crew to Frascati Farm leaving one man in tank 6.30 p.m. On 1 August took my crew back to battle ground and brought tank back to Frascati Farm after an all-night struggle over impossible ground and under shell fire several times.

TANK G3, 2/LT POPPLEWELL

After crossing enemy front line I followed in rear of tanks that were to operate on the Black Line. I then proceeded in front of these tanks to overtake the infantry who were attacking the Black Line. I was then the leading tank, G10 having been ditched, and Capt Powell joined me. I was ditched for 25 minutes in a large shell hole. I put my unditching gear on, but my engine would not pull me out. I went over to G7 [2/Lt Lovell] who towed me out. Whilst I was ditched an infantry subaltern came to me and asked me to give him assistance with a redoubt which was holding him up. On being unditched I proceeded to attack the redoubt, which surrendered at my approach; 60 men and two machine guns being captured. I then made my way towards Canopus Trench in a north-easterly direction from Oblong Farm, intending to cross it to the left of Juliet Farm, but owing to the state of the ground, which had been badly crumped, I had to put on my unditching gear and made my way to the right where I crossed, assisting the infantry in capturing some isolated machine-gunners at Juliet Farm. I then made my way towards St Julien and tried to cross the Steenbeek but was ditched for 45 minutes. I put on my unditching gear but my engine was not strong enough to pull me out. G7 [2/Lt Lovell] was now coming up on my left about 300 yards away. I set my crew to work digging out my sponsons and made my way over to him and asked him for his assistance. He managed to cross the Steenbeek successfully and towed me out – the second time. I then made my way to where the infantry were being held up by a machine-gun emplacement and assisted in capturing 170 prisoners and some

A typical scene on the Flanders front: three Mark IV tanks, a male and two females, hopelessly bogged in the mud.

machine guns and then proceeded again in the direction of my objective and reached the Green Line at 11.00 a.m., finding the infantry consolidated there. I was told by them that machine guns were very active on the left flank. I made off in that direction. At this time I saw G11 [2/Lt Lynch] blown up by a direct hit and about five minutes later G2 [Lt Mawer] was blown up by a direct hit and my own tank was very heavily shelled. We seemed to be under direct observation of a German battery but I was unable to locate its position. Seeing that the two tanks G2 and G11 were beyond help I proceeded on my course and became ditched near St Julien. I put my unditching gear on but was unable to move, so set to work with shovels to try and dig her clear. After working for 50 minutes under very heavy shell and rifle fire the tank was struck by a shell which burst five yards in front, wounding one of my crew and severely shaking three of the others, including myself. I managed to get my crew into a shell hole close by, thoroughly exhausted, whilst I went to G5 [2/Lt Coverdale-Rider] to see if he could tow me as my unditching gear was broken and my clutch burnt out. Finding his tank out of action I started to return when my tank was hit again by a shell, this time a direct hit, which forced me to abandon her.

I cannot speak too highly of the conduct of my crew throughout. Though hopelessly ditched they were very loathe to leave her. Sgt Stockdale and Gnr Davidson showed the greatest courage when ditched and under heavy fire.

TANK G4, LT GARDNER

Left starting point at zero and reached Juliet Farm at zero plus 2.15, when he received news that infantry were held up by machine guns at Canopus and south-east of Kitchener Wood. Became ditched just beyond Juliet and got going again in less than ten minutes. We followed Canopus and did some firing into the redoubt. Result was 20 to 30 enemy surrendered and machine guns silenced. Our infantry were than able to advance. Here enemy surrendered between Canopus and Canteen Trenches. Became ditched just beyond Corner Cot and got out almost at once. Waited under cover for barrage to lift on Black Dotted Line, during which time they filled up with water. On barrage lifting they advanced towards St Julien, firing six pounder over the heads of our infantry into the village. About 100 prisoners came out of St Julien through this fire. Ditched for a third time and while unditching Lewis gun was played on to Winnipeg; unditched in about 20 minutes. On proceeding to cross Steenbeek engaged with six pounder, enemy batteries firing from left and right of Winnipeg. These batteries were silenced. Our infantry were consolidating on Green Dotted Line. River was crossed and then proceeded along the south of the St Julien–Winnipeg road and had to wait for about half an hour for barrage to lift, during which time they replenished the tank. Enemy guns were ranging on to them at this point.

On barrage lifting they advanced towards Winnipeg and became badly ditched in front of concrete gun emplacement. They were two and a half hours getting unditched but were firing indirect fire with the Lewis on to Winnipeg before our infantry got ahead of the tank. The infantry began to retire; unditching gear broke and consequently on account of the ground it was impossible to advance against the machine guns driving the infantry back. They were able to retrace their route back as they got on their old tracks. Lt Gardner led his tank on foot the whole way back, though heavily shelled, and was fired upon near Canteen by enemy aeroplane flying very low, which wounded him.

TANK G3, 2/LT RIDER

Zero hour was at 5.50 a.m. The tank was running well and the crew in good spirits. My tank was to work in pairs with G5 [six pounder] and on its right. I went forward at zero plus 10 and all went well until the second trench of the

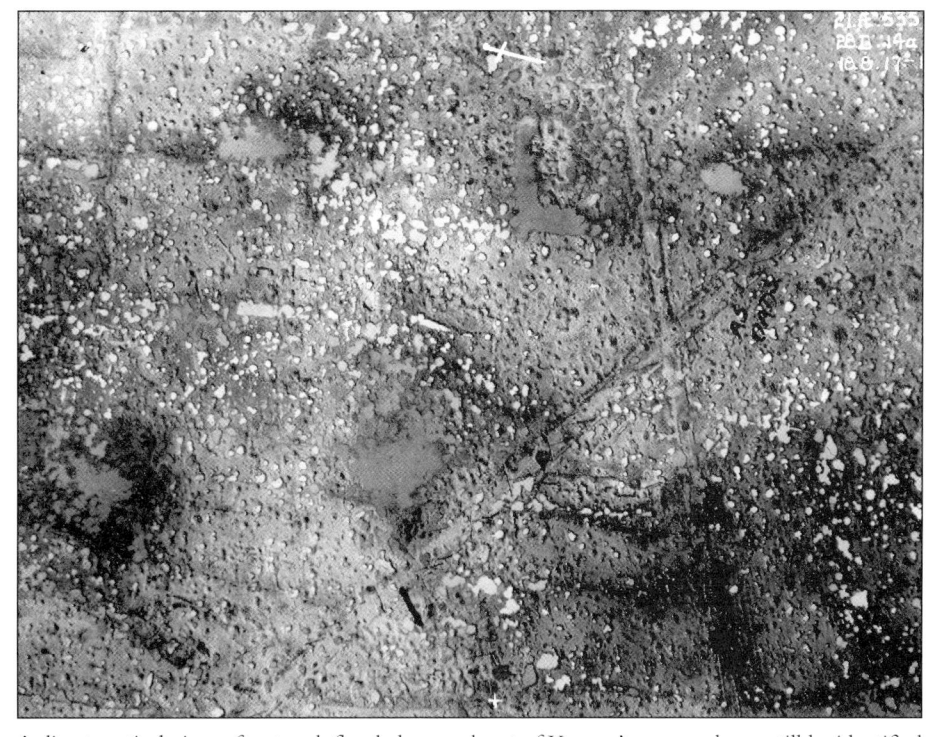

A direct vertical view of cratered, flooded ground east of Ypres. A crossroads can still be identified but there are few other signs to indicate that the area is part of this planet, let alone a part once occupied and farmed.

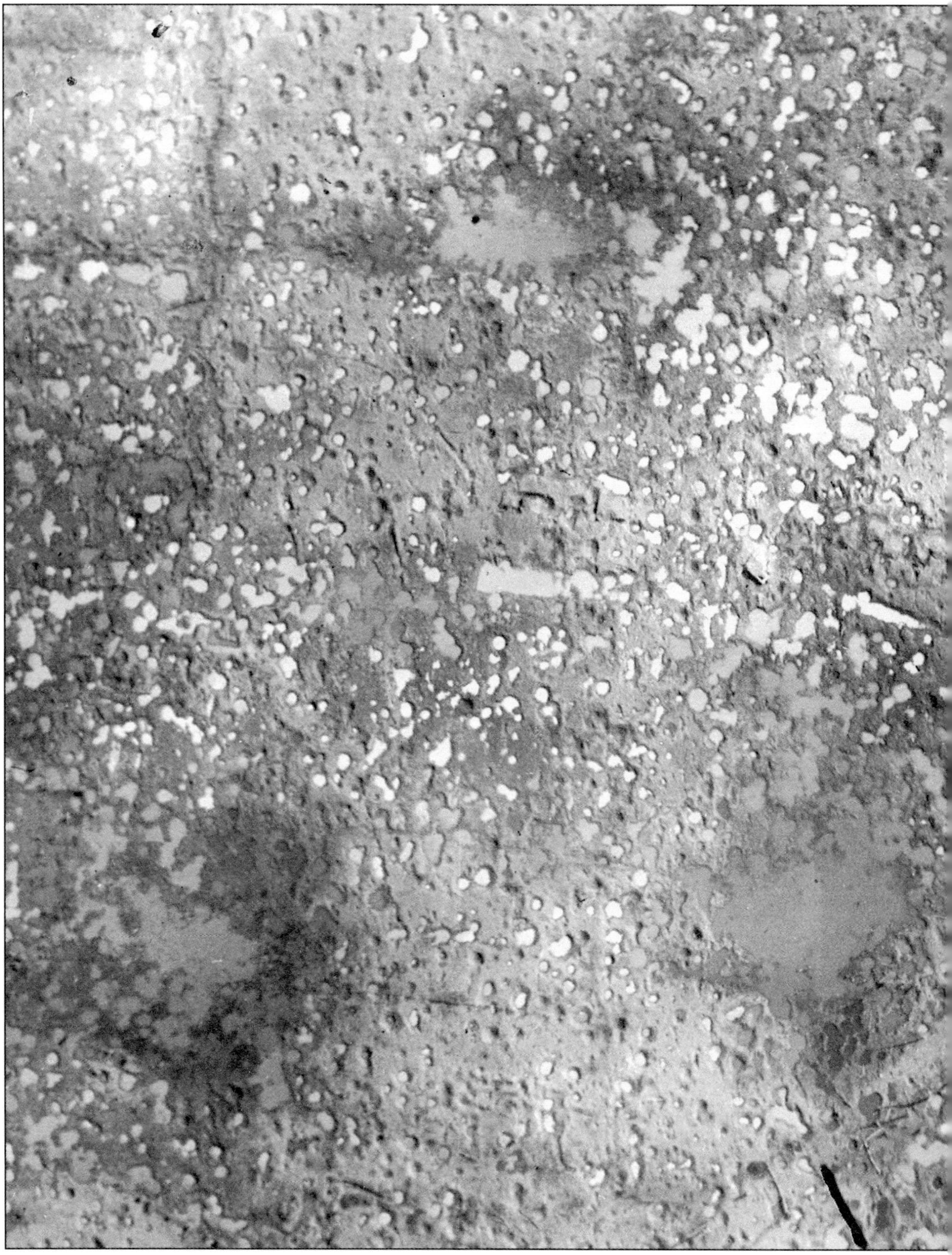

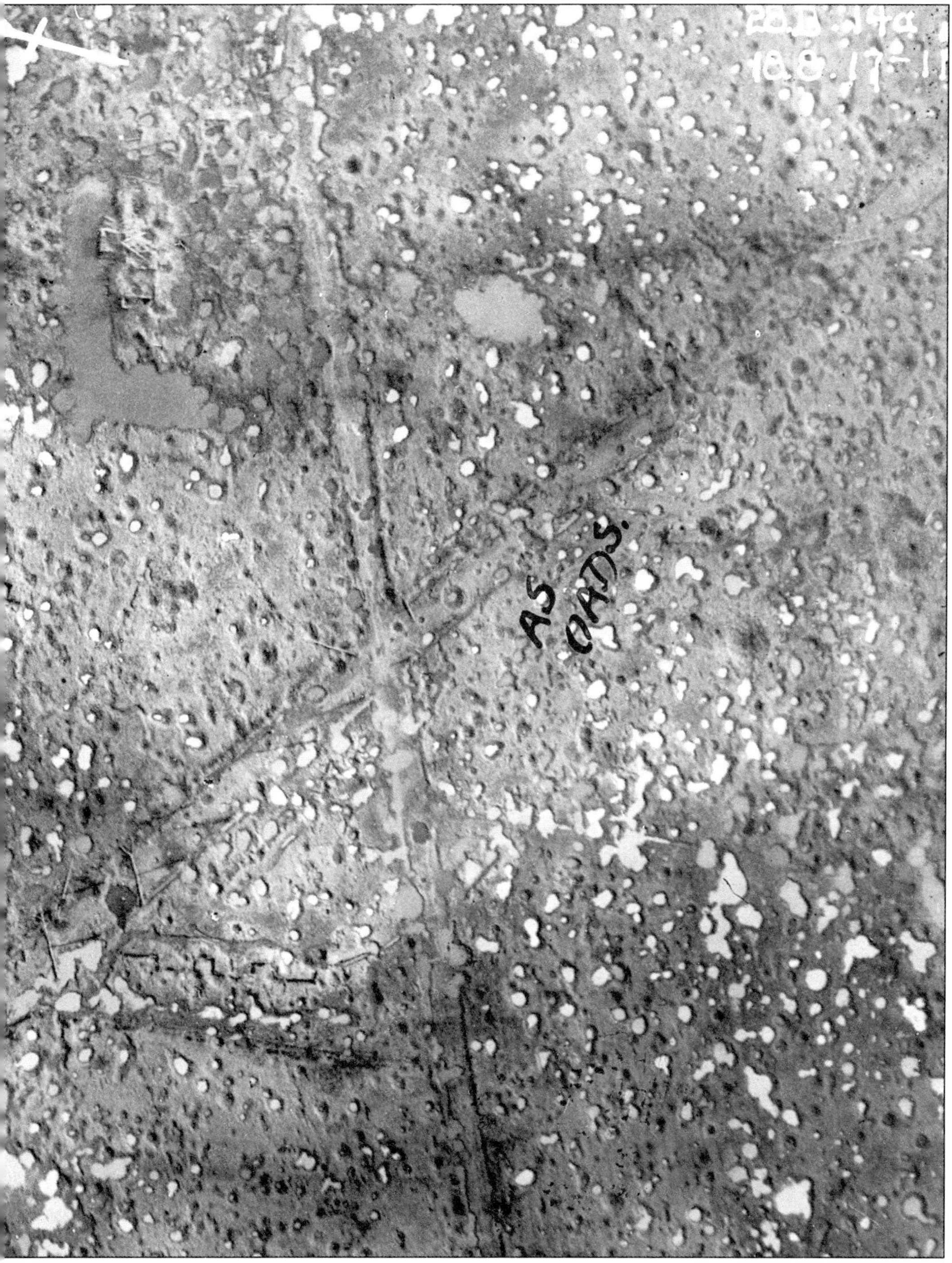

German front system was reached. There my tank was ditched at zero plus 49. By means of the unditching gear and an improvised corduroy road which was manufactured from wood obtained from German trenches, the tank was unditched at zero plus 1.50. Under a heavy enemy barrage I went off in the direction of Oblong Farm and arrived at the Blue Line at zero plus 2.20. At zero plus 2.48 my engine gave out coming out of a shell hole. The engine power was weak owing to the amount of mud on the tracks. This stoppage was almost immediately rectified, but the tank stopped again at zero plus 3.26, through the same cause. The tank was soon got moving again. Canopus Trench was crossed at zero plus 3.28. At zero plus 4.5 the engine was overheating and I stopped and filled the radiator with water obtained from shell holes. On reaching the Alberta–St Julien tram line I kept along it and crossed the Steenbeek at zero plus 4.45. Here I spoke to 2/Lt Popplewell and Lt Mawer, and arranged to patrol up and down the Steenbeek and around St Julien to as far as the Hanebeek with the latter officer.

The infantry were consolidating a line to the St Julien-Poelcapelle road. They were under heavy HE fire and snipers and occasionally machine-gun fire. At

Water-filled shell holes and strongpoints in the German line; features of a landscape in which trench-digging proved impossible.

zero plus 6.47 I was outside my tank to see if it was all alright and to hitch up the unditching gear, which was almost off. I found two holes through my tank under the left side door and one of my guns in the left sponson was smashed in half below the gas regulator key by shrapnel. To my immediate left was a dugout up to which I went. Two of the enemy emerged and I shot them with my revolver for refusing to surrender. The infantry were consolidating a line to the Winnipeg-St Julien road. They were subjected to heavy fire from artillery and machine guns. I went forward to try and find this machine gun, but my tank was only doing about five yards a minute and HE – probably 5.9 shells from several guns in the direction of Springfield – were dropping all around me. At zero plus 7.3 two tanks slightly to my rear were knocked out by shell fire and I determined to take advantage of the cover of a hedge along the Hanebeek river and to approach the enemy and fire upon him. I came through the village of St Julien, over the bridge which was only destroyed in the centre and then bore over towards Border House. I was subjected to point-blank range and under observation from enemy artillery the whole time. My tank got hopelessly ditched. I immediately camouflaged it and sent back a message by pigeon. All attempts to unditch my tank were futile and I went over to 2/Lt Lovell and

Three Mark IVs stuck in the mud and shattered by enemy artillery.

arranged to send five of my crew with four guns to him to help the infantry. I stayed with my tank until zero plus 11.39. The infantry had retired beyond me to the rear of Border House. My two NCOs and I took shelter in a shell hole and I was knocked out for half an hour by a piece of shrapnel; I brought all documents back with me and made for the arranged rallying point but found no section tanks there. I came back and at Wine House helped a company of the Cheshires and Herts (about 90 men) for one and a half hours to consolidate until relieved. I had a Lewis gun with me which was, however, destroyed by shell fire at this place. I left Wine House at zero plus 13.45 and arrived at Frascati at zero plus 15.20.

TANK G7, 2/LT LOVELL

Left starting point at zero and became ditched, but the unditching gear worked splendidly and they became unditched in about ten minutes. Further on they towed out G3 [2/Lt Popplewell] which delayed them about 20 minutes to half an hour. They kept the unditching gear on until they had crossed the Steenbeek, which was done without any difficulty. They then went to G3's assistance as it was ditched in the Steenbeek, smashing their unditching gear soon after. This took about 20 minutes. Enemy guns, probably anti-tank guns because their fire seemed so direct, fired on them from Kansas Cross-Winnipeg direction. The shells came extremely fast, falling very near. They became badly ditched again when it became quite impossible to get the tank out as it had sunk very deep down. This was zero plus 7.20. 2/Lt Lovell went for assistance and was away about 20 minutes. When he returned he ordered the guns to be taken out, together with ten boxes of ammunition (2700 rounds) and put into a shell hole behind. Then with two men he camouflaged the side of the tank facing the enemy and tied the signal 'out of action' on to the top for aeroplane observation. Notices against looting from the tank were hung up and the tank locked up. When he had made his strongpoints 2/Lt Lovell returned alone to the tank and finished the camouflage. A Taube flew very low over them soon after, dropping a light. They fired on it with a Lewis gun and one man with his revolver. After three quarters of an hour the infantry [the Cambridgeshires] seemed to be held up and so the crew went forward 100 yards, during which journey Lt Lovell was hit whilst carrying two boxes of ammunition. He remained an hour on duty, during which time the remainder of the crew made a strongpoint of shell holes. All our infantry except 15, consisting of Cheshires, Lancashire Fusiliers and Cambridgeshires, had retired from here. The 20 of them made three strongpoints with four Lewis guns. They silenced a machine gun near derelict G2. Several enemy were killed from their fire. Taubes again flew over and dropped lights near their infantry and swooped down towards our outposts. Result was a big whizz-bang barrage. The crew therefore decided to remove 2/Lt Lovell so four of them went back with him. Cpl Crawshaw, GnrHiggins and Gnr Coultas remained at their guns, handing the fourth over to the Cambridgeshires.

These three men remained in their strong points for two more hours, until they had finished the whole of their ammunition, their chief targets being the Cemetery and encircling to the right towards G2 tank. A company runner came up and said a party of 200 was coming up to relieve them, but they did not arrive and as the Germans were counterattacking in large numbers behind a heavy barrage, Cpl Crawshaw gave the order about 5 p.m. to retire. They recrossed the Steenbeek and dropped into the line which had been dug by the Hertfordshires and Cambridgeshires. Cpl Crawshaw then went to Frascati, having lost Coultas and Higgins, reaching it at 10 p.m.

Coultas and Higgins, however, had joined up with the infantry and were given rifles. They remained at their posts with the infantry until dawn, when they were relieved by the Sussex Regiment. They reached Frascati at 8 a.m. The whole crew is loud in their praise for 2/Lt Lovell, who risked all dangers himself rather than allow his men to do so. He encouraged them so long as he had sufficient strength and they attributed largely to his example that they stuck to their posts.

TANK G9, 2/LT MAELOR-JONES

From Halfway House to Frascati. On this journey the tank gave much trouble in reaching Frascati Wood owing to the engine knocking badly. The following day Workshops took it in hand and later reported it fit. Later in the day we discovered that the radiator was leaking. After tightening the envelope it apparently ceased to leak.

From Frascati to Starting Point. Just after starting the engine stopped but was started again and proceeded quite well to the starting point.

At dawn on 31 July I proceeded with other tanks of No. 3 Section, crossing over the enemy front line in a north-easterly direction for Kitchener Wood to the right of the Oblong and Juliet Farms. At the latter I waited for our barrage to lift, meanwhile filling up the radiator with water. I then steered for Alberta, leaving it on my left. Here I met some Hampshires retiring. With difficulty I persuaded a man to speak. He told me they were held up by machine guns. I advanced towards a long blockhouse about six feet high where I observed a machine-gun emplacement on which I drove the tank. On the other side I came on a machine gun and two men whom we shot [2/Lt Maelor-Jones shot

A German strongpoint in reinforced concrete with a field gun dug in for anti-tank use, now in British hands.

one with his revolver, opening his window to do so] and crumpled up the gun. Advancing we came upon an old and strong breastwork manned by the enemy on which our gunners opened fire. The Hampshires then came on and cleared the trench, taking all prisoners. On our right a number of prisoners were taken. We advanced towards the Steenbeek, filling a few cans with water on the way. We struck the trench tramway and followed it to the crossing at Steenbeek. I found the tram bridge incapable of taking a tank. I then cruised along the Steenbeek until the engine began to give trouble. We put all available water in under heavy shell fire and decided we should have to return. We made for the north-east side of Kitchener Wood where we refilled with water from shell holes. I proceeded as far as the north corner where we had to refill again. Steering round the north-west of the wood we got 300 yards when the engine refused to pull. We refilled again under heavy shell fire, after which we reached Hurst Park where the engine refused to take the ground. After making several vain attempts to assist the tracks by putting timber and earth underneath I decided to report the situation to company headquarters. I therefore closed the tank and camouflaged the top with mud. I returned with the crew and reported to my company commander. After the crew had had a meal at Frascati I returned to the tank with four men and remained until relieved the following day at 5.50 p.m.

TANK G11, 2/LT LYNCH

Information obtained from eyewitnesses as far as possible.

> Left starting point and went well as far as Black Line where they caught up the infantry and advanced with them up to and over the Steenbeek. Between 8.45 and 9.15 a.m. the tank was seen cruising about on the Green Dotted Line and was firing from the guns on its left sponson, and also from the front. Between 9.15 and 9.50 a.m. the tank was seen to be firing in a stationary position and was at this time near G10. The tank then proceeded towards Springfield and was under very heavy shell fire the whole way. The guns from the ridge to the right seemed to be ranging on it, from direct observation. At about 11.15 a.m. a shell struck the centre of the tank, enveloping it in a 30 yard circle of smoke. When the smoke cleared only the mere outline of the tank could be seen.

It has not been possible to ascertain what assistance this tank was able to render to the infantry up to the Steenbeek, but beyond this point it appears to have been busily engaged and advancing directly towards its final objective. 2/Lt Lynch and the whole of his crew were killed.

TANK G45, LT MERCHANT

The tank was in position at the starting point at 3.40 a.m. on 31 July. At zero we moved slowly forward and crossed our own front line and negotiated the enemy front line which had been completely destroyed by fire. No landmarks were visible and we steered entirely by compass. We were ditched just afterwards but got out in seven minutes with the aid of the heavy unditching gear. Steering north, north-east we had no more trouble and made out Lone Tree and Kitchener Wood and were able to keep to our route. Nearing Bosche Castel we skirted the wet ground and passed G46, which was going well. The infantry were just in front at this point and my section commander warned me of machine-gun fire from Kitchener Wood which was holding up the infantry. The ground round Bosche Castel strongpoint was very badly crumped by 15 inch guns, and in swinging half-right to get on to this machine gun the tank stuck in a crater. I decided to try the unditching gear without digging as we were so near to the infantry, and time was everything. The gear was fixed under

A severely ditched Mark IV female with the unditching beam still in place. If the tank was still functioning, and the crew alive, this beam would be attached to the tracks and used to lever the tank out of its predicament.

extreme difficulty owing to sniper fire from both sides. The engine was labouring badly and would not pull the boom round. We then dug the sponson clear of the clay and tried again, but the engine would not pull and developed a bad knock. A pigeon message was sent off at 10.15 a.m. to this effect and the crew stood by the tank. We were under heavy shell fire all day and thought that we had been spotted, despite the camouflage, by a Taube which passed over at 3 p.m. At 8 p.m. a guard was mounted in case of a counterattack, as it was our idea to take up a defensive position with the Lewis guns if necessary. Rain came on very heavily and we passed a very unpleasant night being shelled incessantly. We had practically no rations. At 9.50 a.m. on the following morning the Salvage Officer came up and under his instructions we built a ramp and tried to run the tank backwards. The engine again knocked badly and the Salvage Officer agreed that serious engine trouble was there, probably a sleeve or big end gone. I reported fully by runner to my section commander at 12 o'clock and the crew still stood by. At 4 p.m., having received no further order, owing to the exhausted state of the crew and the continuous shelling, I decided to evacuate. 2/Lt Browne, whose tank G46 was ditched 200 yards north of my tank, agreed with me in this decision and we withdrew our crews and guns to Frascati, locking up both tanks. The crew behaved splendidly throughout a very trying period.

TANK G46, 2/LT BROWNE

I moved off from starting point at zero on the morning of 31 July. It was then very dark and no landmarks were visible. Following the next ahead, G45, I crossed our front line and no-man's land without difficulty but found the enemy front line very badly smashed about, with a great deal of water. It took me half an hour to cross, great assistance being given by my section commander who guided me from outside. Having crossed I saw a tank on fire to my right. I passed G45 temporarily ditched and shortly after, visibility having improved, I saw Lone Tree and steered straight for it. My unditching gear and camouflage carried away, the lashing apparently having been cut by shrapnel from the enemy's barrage. Being behind time I did not wait to pick them up. I was able then, without much difficulty, to reach the enemy trenches in front of Kitchener Wood. G45 now passed me on the left and became ditched at Bosche Castel. I moved along the front of the wood, crossed the road and trench tramway running past the north end and then turned north-east parallel to the road. At this time I got off a few rounds at some of the enemy left behind our infantry in Kitchener Wood and at a machine-gun emplacement in Von Werder House. The ground here was extremely bad – waterlogged and full of shell holes with water. I tried to get back on to the road which I had been warned to keep off if possible as it was mined, but I found I could only go straight forward. The tank was so deep in that it would neither swing nor reverse, and after moving forward about 200 yards it became ditched in a shell hole full of water. The water immediately poured in over the floor boards. I endeavoured to improvise unditching gear with beams, concrete blocks and my spare chains but found it impossible to move the tank. The clutch would not work, having apparently been affected by the water, which was now nearly a foot deep on the left side. The machine gun in Von Werder House had been firing at me but now ceased. No enemy troops were visible and I was informed by our infantry that they were back to, or across, the Steenbeek. At 8.30 a.m. I sent back a pigeon message to report my condition. I then went over to G45 where I found my section commander. At 10.30, in accordance with his orders, I sent five of my crew with my NCO back to report to Company HQ, remaining myself in the tank with one gunner. About this time I gave some drums of ammunition to the infantry. It now began to rain and the whole area round my tank became flooded. In the course of the afternoon my crew returned, having been ordered to stand by the tank. One man was hit on the way back. The enemy had now begun to shell the ground around Bosche Castel heavily, and this shelling continued throughout the day and night. I think it possible that my tank, with G45, was spotted by an enemy aeroplane which flew over very low at 2 p.m. We were shelled heavily all night and the water continued to rise in the tank. The following morning the Salvage Officer arrived and at his suggestion I endeavoured to bale out the pool but without any effect. I then removed the magneto and put it in the locker to keep it dry. At 4 o'clock in the afternoon, having received no orders, having exhausted all my water and most of the rations, being still under continual shell fire and finding that my crew was completely exhausted and wet through after 30 hours up to their knees in water, I consulted with Lt Merchant of G45 and we decided to lock up the tanks and withdraw. We reached Frascati about 6 p.m. that afternoon.

TANK G47, 2/LT ALLDEN

We left our starting point (Bilge Trench) about 3.56 a.m. on 31 July. There was a little delay somewhere in front which prevented us from moving at 3.50. A

Lt Browne's tank G46, sunk up to its sponsons. The right track has broken and peeled backwards.

tank on our left cannoned into us as we went forward. After going about 60 yards we found tank G48 on our left but immediately we divided owing to a tank being in our path. I went to the right of this tank and G48 went to the left. This was the last I saw of this tank until after the action.

When I had crossed the British trenches, which caused me no trouble, I went forward as fast as I could. Soon after this a corporal of the Sherwoods came towards the tank and cautioned me as to the ground on my right. I therefore went a bit to the left and was able to see that the ground I was warned against was very boggy. I had been unable to see it from the front owing to the smoke and dust. After this we noticed a lot of smoke in the tank. Pyrenes [fire extinguishers] were soon obtained and we searched for the cause of the smoke. A private shouted that we were on fire on top so I told my sergeant and Gnr Eagles to get out with me and we removed the camouflage which was on fire on the top. After going on for some little distance we had our unditching gear blown away by a shell and we did not trouble to put it on again. Having passed Oblong Farm we made straight for the middle of Kitchener Wood, on which the barrage seemed to be still playing. Here we were able to engage an enemy machine gun and I put a magazine and a half into the position and this had the effect of silencing the gun. I now turned south-east and travelled along Kitchener Wood. My gunners (Nos 1 and 3) were on the lookout for targets but saw little. We went to the corner of the wood and then reversed, and went back along it again, still firing occasionally. As we saw no decent targets we made for our corner again and, having reached it, turned north-east towards Alberta, and now I had plenty of opportunity of using my guns again. There were many of the enemy running for their lives up communication trenches and I stopped some or hastened their flight. A machine gun was seen on my right and after changing my gun for the spare one I was able to quieten this, and soon after I saw some prisoners with a machine gun being moved from here to our infantry. All this time guns Nos 1 and 3 were firing into the wood whenever they saw a sign of the fleeing enemy. I now came across some of the officers of the 17th Sherwoods. I got to know them before we left Oosthoek and we agreed to look out for each other. They were very glad to see us and told us that Alberta was straight ahead. We went on, and what appeared to be a machine gun was engaged on the left. After this I got a little too far to the right and was soon in our barrage. I straightened up a bit and made for Alberta, in front of which I saw the 17th Sherwoods who were waiting for the barrage to lift and for the machine guns at Alberta to be silenced. I travelled along three sides of Alberta and poured in a good fire, and as our own barrage had not lifted yet we reversed and went round the three sides again. Three machine guns were certainly engaged about here, two in the strongpoint itself, and one on the right. We all had a chance of shooting. About this time five of our six guns were out of action and I was able to fire through the front flap with my revolver and it must have had good effect for when the barrage lifted the infantry were able to go to the strongpoint without any resistance and we soon saw a party with machine guns come out and return towards our lines as prisoners. The 17th Sherwoods at once consolidated and I sent my first pigeon off.

While moving about Alberta we became ditched. It was not a large shell hole but our engine had very little power and was unable to pull us out. We all got out and dug away while the enemy shells were bursting all around us in their endeavour to strafe Alberta. The men behaved splendidly but we could not dig the tank out. At this point a runner from the Sherwoods came up to us and told us where the HQ of Capt Miller was. We obtained help from some Sherwoods who tried to dig us out but again failed. Then I took my guns and some ammunition and went to Capt Miller.

We stayed a little while and then, seeing a tank in the distance, I went and asked the commander [2/Lt Jordan] to help pull me out. The crew and guns were got back into the tank and an attempt made to pull us out. It failed, and I decided to be pulled in the hole a little more so as to be less conspicuous to the enemy. This was done and I then put up my signal – three reds – but had no response. I did not put the white cloth on top because a Boche plane was hovering near. I then detailed my sergeant and one man to stay by the tank as guard, and taking guns and the remainder of the crew, one of which had been wounded when trying to unditch and another in a state of collapse, we made for Hill Top to get orders. I was told that a counterattack was expected and was advised to get back with my guns and dig in. Having left my two sick men behind, the remainder of us went back again and after getting the guns cleaned again we once more tried to develop more power from the engine, and through a suggestion of my sergeant's we did so, with the result that after more digging we were able to get out of the hole. We at once made for our rallying point where we stayed all night. I sent off my second pigeon next morning and at about 1 p.m. I was able to move again. After six hours' journey we reached Hill Top where we received a message from Capt Kessell telling us to report to Frascati and leave a man on guard over the tank. We did this and reached Frascati after being with the tank for close on 45 hours. All were very much exhausted. Sgt Brown and Gnr Eagles deserve special mention.

TANK G26 (CABLE-CARRYING TANK), 2/LT KILLOY

This tank left Frascati ten minutes after zero on 31 July, my objectives for dumping cables being (i) the junction of Calf Avenue and Calf Reserve Trench and (ii) Corner Cot. The journey to my first objective was uneventful.

A Mark IV female tank and signallers laying a cable, photographed near Hooge on 20 September 1917.

The signal personnel which should have reported to me at Frascati three hours before zero did not put in an appearance, and as I had no orders as to how much cable was to be dumped at each point I dumped half at the Calf Junction and the remainder at the second point, there being eight cable reels in all. On proceeding to my second objective I was heavily shelled and eventually had to drop the remainder of the cables at 17 Central – no Royal Engineers or Divisional Signallers being at hand anywhere to take it over – the same being the case at my first point.

On my return journey I was ditched in the old German third line, getting out, however, with my unditching gear after an hour's work. Proceeding I was ordered by Maj. Fernie, OC XIX Company, to assist a XXI Company tank – 2/Lt Brassington – to get unditched, and succeeded in hauling this tank out. I got the tank back to Frascati at 3.30 p.m.

SUPPLY TANK GS2, LT WILLARD

At about 9.15 p.m. on 30 July I left Halfway House near Frascati Farm for Frascati, which I reached about 3.30 a.m. I then covered up the tank and awaited orders. A few hours later, the horse transport having failed to get

A supply tank, a Mark I male with its guns removed and the sponsons sheeted over to contain stores. This one was photographed during the Messines battle, earlier in the Flanders campaign.

forward, I was warned to be ready to move as soon as possible. Spuds [see picture on p. 27] were put on and the tank got ready to move off.

At about 12 noon I was ordered to proceed to the Refilling Point. There was no difficulty in following the tracks of the fighting tanks and we crossed our own and the German lines without difficulty. We were stopped once just before reaching our front line owing to the filler cap of the radiator breaking and allowing the water to escape. We improvised a plug and were able to proceed after about 20 minutes. When this happened I at once sent a man back to report to Capt Rudd at Frascati and endeavour to get a new filler cap. This he brought to me later when we were at Canadian Farm. Beyond Canadian Farm we took the track of the right-hand tank and in a few minutes I met Capt Chadwick who told me it was useless to make a dump at the original filling point as it would certainly be destroyed. He told me to go to a line of pollard willows and there camouflage until I received definite orders. Almost as soon as I had camouflaged the tank I received a message from Maj. Fernie ordering me to go to Kultur Farm and refill two tanks there. Just before I moved off I received another order from Maj. Fernie to make a dump at Kultur Farm and then return empty to Frascati. On the way to Kultur Farm I was ditched about 100 yards south of it and was unable to extricate the tank. Capt Winters then came and ordered me to leave one man on the tank and take the rest back to Frascati. Just before we left some oil was drawn from the supplies in the tank by 2/Lt Brassington.

On 1 August petrol was drawn by 2/Lt Allden and 2/Lt Jordan, and in the evening I took the crew and a small labour party and made a dump near the tank with all the stores in the tank except the small arms ammunition which I was told to leave in the tank. I did not unditch the tank, however, as the state of the ground was so bad, though in drier weather I was sure it would have come out fairly easily. As the action went on the weather and ground became rapidly worse. The hostile shelling was fairly light and spread pretty evenly over the whole piece of country I could see. On the night of 2 August the last man was withdrawn from the tank which is still ditched, but undamaged.

1ST GUN CARRIER COMPANY, SEPTEMBER 1917

A Section was formed at Leeds on 9 July 1917, under the command of Lt E.M. Brown. After a period of training, which included practice in tank driving and mounting and dismounting of guns at Leeds, and experimental firing at Shoeburyness, they embarked for France on 31 August 1917. On arrival at Erin training was continued until 6 September 1917, when they drew six gun-carrier tanks from Central Workshops and proceeded by train to Ouderdon, where they came under the supervision of Maj. Dick, who was in command of the workshops of 2nd Tank Brigade. While here further experimental work was carried out, in the progress of which it became apparent that, owing to mechanical trouble and the nature of the ground, the tails – as then fitted to the tanks – were undesirable. These were accordingly abandoned before actual carrying operations commenced. After resting at Ouderdon for three days, the section was split up, HQ remaining at Ouderdon, four tanks proceeding to Zillebeke and two to Three Kilo Point (near Woodcote House), where they were employed in carrying 6 in. howitzers and sixty pounder guns and ammunition.

The section was soon to experience the horrors of war, as tank GC102 received a direct hit from a 5.9 shell which caused nine casualties. With the exception of Cpl James, who recovered from his wounds and subsequently rejoined the Tank Corps, all were killed outright or mortally wounded.

D BATTALION, 18 SEPTEMBER 1917

No. 12 Company was again chosen for the coming attack, which was to be on a large scale on practically the whole salient front. In the late afternoon of

Although taken in 1918, this picture of the Gun-Carrier *Darlington* is typical. It shows the 6 in. howitzer in its cradle at the front, between the driver's and commander's cabs. The gun wheels are slung at the sides and extra ammunition stowed everywhere.

18 September four sections, including the supply section No. 11, left Oosthoek and trekked forward by the same route as previously, via Brielen to Murat farm, where the night was spent. But the proximity of a large 12 in. railway gun effectively did away with any idea of continuous sleep.

The three fighting sections took fills of oil, grease, petrol, etc. from the supply sections and then moved forward to their final lying-up places. No. 9 section under Capt Smith had to make for St Julien and Nos 10 and 12 sections for Rudolphe Farm some 1,000 yd east of Pilckem. The journey was carried out in the dark and the congestion on the roads forward made the journey an exciting yet wearisome one. Streams of traffic in both directions on a 30 ft road do not tend to make things run smoothly, and the battle went naturally to the strong. Dozens of horse limbers were pushed into the ditches at the side of the road and artillery and transport men cursed the tanks. But before dawn the three sections had reached their destinations and were camouflaged up as well as possible among the rubble of one-time farms with brick-coloured camouflage nets which they carried.

The 19th was spent quietly and with many a prayer that the enemy would not see through the scanty camouflage. Night arrived and final overhauls were made

Camouflaged tanks on the battlefield, with infantry moving past. Although obvious from ground level, they would be well disguised from the air.

in complete silence, darkness and steady rain. Then, shortly before zero, 5.30 a.m. on the 20th, all tanks moved into battle positions. The company was to attack with the 51st Highland Division from the Pilckem Ridge in the direction of Poelcapelle, with the 58th London Division on the right completing the Corps front. There are few things so nerve-racking as waiting for the attack; the suspense of inaction made the arrival of zero almost welcome.

Nos 10 and 12 sections were again to experiment with a cross-country attack over ground which was thought to be less pounded than usual, with Kangaroo Avenue, Rose House and Delta House, all to the west of Poelcapelle, as final objectives. The optimism was not justified. A few of the early objectives were reached and captured without difficulty, but before long tank after tank became completely stuck, two receiving direct hits, and not one succeeded in reaching the final objective.

No. 9 section was only slightly more fortunate. The four tanks were to move up the Poelcapelle road in file and deploy on reaching the Lekkerbotterbeek stream. The rear tank (Lt R.A. Jones) was knocked out before leaving St Julien village, but the remaining three pushed on as fast as possible up the road, only to

A knocked-out Mark IV female lies abandoned near a dug-in forward dressing station.

find it strewn with felled trees and other obstacles. In crossing one of the trees the second tank sideslipped and ditched badly at the side of the road, effectively barring the progress of the third tank, which was unable to make its way either over the tree or round the second tank. The leading car, under Lt Symonds, went on to perform almost superhuman deeds in the two miles to Poelcapelle. It surmounted all obstacles, only to find the road become a swamp. By means of continuous ramping the tank was kept in line with the infantry and rendered valuable assistance with its guns, and only on arrival at the outskirts of the village did the engine break down and leave the crew stranded. The tank was then held as a strongpoint till such time as the 51st Division had consolidated. For this action Lt Symonds was awarded the MC and the crew one MM and two Belgian Croix de Guerre.

D BATTALION, 4 OCTOBER 1917

This was the date of one of the most successful tank actions of the whole 1917 Flanders campaign. The object of the attack was the capture and subjection of

A knocked-out Mark IV on the Poelcapelle road. Only heavy artillery is likely to have caused such damage, and it could just as easily have come from a British barrage.

the village and surroundings of Poelcapelle, which had been strongly fortified by the enemy in view of tank attacks. No. 10 Company, under Capt Maris, was detailed for the show and they had the unenviable knowledge that the ground to be covered had been shelled without cessation for two months. Their only hope lay in keeping to the St Julien-Poelcapelle road, but they were fully aware of the fact that the Germans would keep an almost impassable barrage on this particular route. Luck, however, was on the side of the Tank Corps for once, and eleven out of twelve successfully manoeuvred through the barrage to the village streets. Here they found the going better and, deploying in Poelcapelle, were the decisive factor in its capture. They then pushed on to the outskirts and completed the destruction of all adjacent strongpoints.

On 9 October two sections of Maj. Watson's No. 11 Company, under captains Talbot and Skinner, participated in a small, local attack. In this instance luck deserted them, the two leading tanks receiving direct hits on the road up and, being unable to move further, they completely blocked the road for the remainder. The last tank then ditched, so the rest were caught in a trap in which they were subjected to a heavy barrage which finally accounted for the lot, and the attack served to swell the huge number of derelict tanks in the salient.

A water-carrying party walking down the track of a field tramway past a ditched Mark IV female near the Zillebeke stream on 20 September 1917.

Male and female Mark IV tanks in a shattered wood at Jackdaw Switch on the Zonnebeke in September 1917.

One branch of the Corps deserves special mention for very gallant work done in a very quiet way. The Tank Salvage Companies had the thankless job of recovering every possible salvageable portion of every derelict tank as promptly as possible. Those who served in the salient know that the task was tremendous, with all the kicks and no ha'pence. After every action the position of each ditched or otherwise immovable tank was reported to the Tank Salvage Company, who had to set to work immediately, whatever the position of the tank, which often meant salvaging on the actual front line. The results achieved are sufficient proof of the gallantry and efficiency of this branch of the Corps, and the rewards they received were fully deserved, as tank salvage was by no means the cushy job that many imagined.

October was near its end when news of a move came through and, finally, orders for entrainment. A tank battalion on the move was always reminiscent of a tortoise, in that it had to carry its home about with it. No rows of comfortable hutments were allotted it in the new area and tank trains carried not only the machines themselves but tents, tarpaulins, duckboards, pit props, floor boarding, wire beds, etc., and anything that made for increased comfort. And so it was that on the evening of 30 October, when we bade farewell to the salient, our train more resembled a timber dump than a mobile fighting unit. And at midnight we rumbled out of Belgium into France.

CHAPTER FOUR

Cambrai

The Battle of Cambrai, which is still celebrated by the Royal Tank Regiment, marks the coming of age of the Tank Corps. Its very scale presented the new arm with a major logistical challenge. Moving the tanks to the battlefront, fitting them all with the newly devised fascines and then keeping them supplied over an extensive battlefield are factors that many histories overlook. Revolutionary and successful as it was, even this surprise attack did not finish the war. The Germans reacted swiftly and to great effect, while the British, ill-prepared for such success, failed to exploit it and soon lost nearly every gain.

At Cambrai the Tank Corps committed nine battalions, fielding a total of 378 Mark IV tanks with fifty-four more held in reserve. Most of these were equipped with the huge fascines which were used as stepping stones over the wider trenches. Extra tanks were equipped as wire-cutters to deal with barbed wire, while others served as mobile wireless stations or carried supplies.

QM STAFF, CAPT C. WEAVER PRICE, 20 NOVEMBER 1917

As Staff Captain (Q) of HQ Tank Corps, the instructions given me about fourteen days before the battle were to supervise the concentration of over 300 tanks at the Plateau siding (near Albert and close to The Loop siding where we assembled in September 1916). The tanks, with personnel, arriving on trains were quickly placed under cover of woods, necessary repairs and adjustments made and, finally, loaded on trains for dispatch to their several kicking-off points for battle. On account of fear of observation by the enemy the whole detraining and entraining had to be done during darkness, even torches and Helleson lamps being used very sparingly. I wish space would allow me to attempt a word picture of the scene of a night when company after company of tanks would creep out of cover and crawl to their respective ramps, but I must be content to merely record that the whole scheme was successfully carried out. But not without some terribly anxious times. The very first train scheduled to arrive was delayed several hours through the rear coaches running off the line, causing deaths and injuries to personnel. One very serious trouble was the gradual collapse of the special trucks for carrying tanks. They had been previously

A long tank train getting ready to depart. Moving the mass of tanks down from Flanders and then despatching them secretly to the Cambrai area was a massive task.

subjected to much hard wear, as their switchback appearance indicated, and only the most optimistic of us thought they would last the job out. Several had to be scrapped but, thank Heavens, enough held together to hurry up the last tank. During the twelve days or so I was at Plateau my working hours were 9 a.m. to 7 a.m. and on three occasions I worked right through the twenty four.

For the actual battle I was engaged in rushing up spare guns, ammunition, petrol, etc. Although that organizing genius, Col. Uzielle, had arranged a most perfect system for replenishment of supplies by light railways, at times even this proved inadequate and lorries were brought into use. I always had a great admiration for the men of the Ammunition Supply Columns. It appeared to me that their work called for more control of nerves than even – say – waiting to go over the top, or serving machine guns in a Holdfast at dawn, in anticipation of an attack by the enemy. This task of mine confirmed my views and ever after I sympathized with a column, waiting patiently for the enemy to cease plastering the road ahead; a perfectly nerve-racking ordeal.

The battle having been gloriously won, new plans for exploiting the success necessitated postponement of the long sleep I had promised myself. At 5 a.m. on the following day I started in my car to collect more emergency supplies and convoy them to Ribecourt and Marcoing, which were then in our hands. Followed by six lorries packed with 6 pdr shells, petrol, etc. I set out on my journey with the idea of delivering the goods and being back at Albert in time for dinner. Vain hope! At 6 p.m. we had only reached Metz and I was here solemnly warned by the APM not to be fool enough to attempt getting through. As my orders were to 'Get Through' I had to ignore his counsel and so pushed on to Trescault. These few miles occupied hours in traversing, congestion was not the word for it – four lines of traffic, two up and two down, with frequent blocks. At length Trescault was reached, and the scene here beggars description. I shall never forget the Jock private who was the sole representative of the traffic control people. If the reader will try to visualize The Bank★ at the busiest time of day, and then imagine *one* policeman attempting to regulate all the traffic he will have a faint idea of what that Kiltie was doing – and really doing it well. Punctuated with shouted orders to drivers of all description of vehicles he told me that all roads forward were 'done in by Jerry'. I left him swinging his lantern, the only light allowed on the patch.

I decided to temporarily park the lorries up a cutting while I went ahead to see how the land lay. I discovered that the enemy had blown up the road and, what was worse, our cavalry had picked up the hard surface, exposing the putty-like substance underneath. Lorry traffic was out of the question. My map showed an alternative route through Havrincourt and this I resolved to try. A good hour was spent in extricating the lorries from the mess up in Trescault but finally we got going well towards Havrincourt. Alas and alack, we struck another crater made by the enemy and we were now properly checked – good and hard! Fortunately at Trescault I had bumped into Lt Bainbridge, who was my assistant at Headquarters. He had been sent up from Central Stores with a lorry of machine guns, so we joined forces and had a good solid think. Just before dawn we evolved a scheme which we at once commenced carrying out. The supplies were dumped in a field off the roadside, a guard was borrowed from a divisional ammunition column, the lorries were sent home, while we proceeded to Ribecourt via Metz. Here we made arrangements with 3rd Brigade for tanks to make a cross-country journey to pick up the goods. This was successfully done and, thirty nine hours after leaving it, I reported to HQ at Albert. Next day I was told that, owing to a change of plans, the supplies were not required! But in the meantime I had put in 16 hours of dreamless sleep, so nothing mattered.

★ The Bank; junction of Threadneedle Street, Cornhill, Lombard Street, King William Street, Queen Victoria Street, Poultry and Princes Street in the City of London.

CAMBRAI

An oblique view of the Cambrai battlefield looking north-west. The earthworks of the Canal du Nord show up clearly on the left, with the German front line in the foreground and the Hindenburg Line marked where it crosses Route Nationale 29 leading to Cambrai (off picture right). The dark mass of Bourlon Wood is visible beyond the road. Compared with the Ypres area, this looks positively civilized.

F Battalion: Preparations for Cambrai

On 19 September a party proceeded to Erin to draw new tanks to replace casualties of the Ypres battle, thus bringing the battalion back up to fighting strength.

The workshop personnel, assisted by the crews, started a systematic overhaul of all tanks. They were jacked up on sleepers, the tracks broken and the Flanders mud scraped out from the rollers and switches. Those tanks not on the stocks went out daily under their section officers, training the drivers and crews. Great attention was paid to getting the men to use their judgement in the choice of ground, when wanting to cross a trench system. On the maintenance and mechanical side the aim was to get the men to rely more upon themselves, so that the workshops were only called upon to help in work of the most technical character.

Quarry Wood.
ARRAS - CAM
ROUTE NATLE NO
E27d.50:79
k9c
Lock No7.
CANAL UNDER CONSTRUCTION
poil
eap.

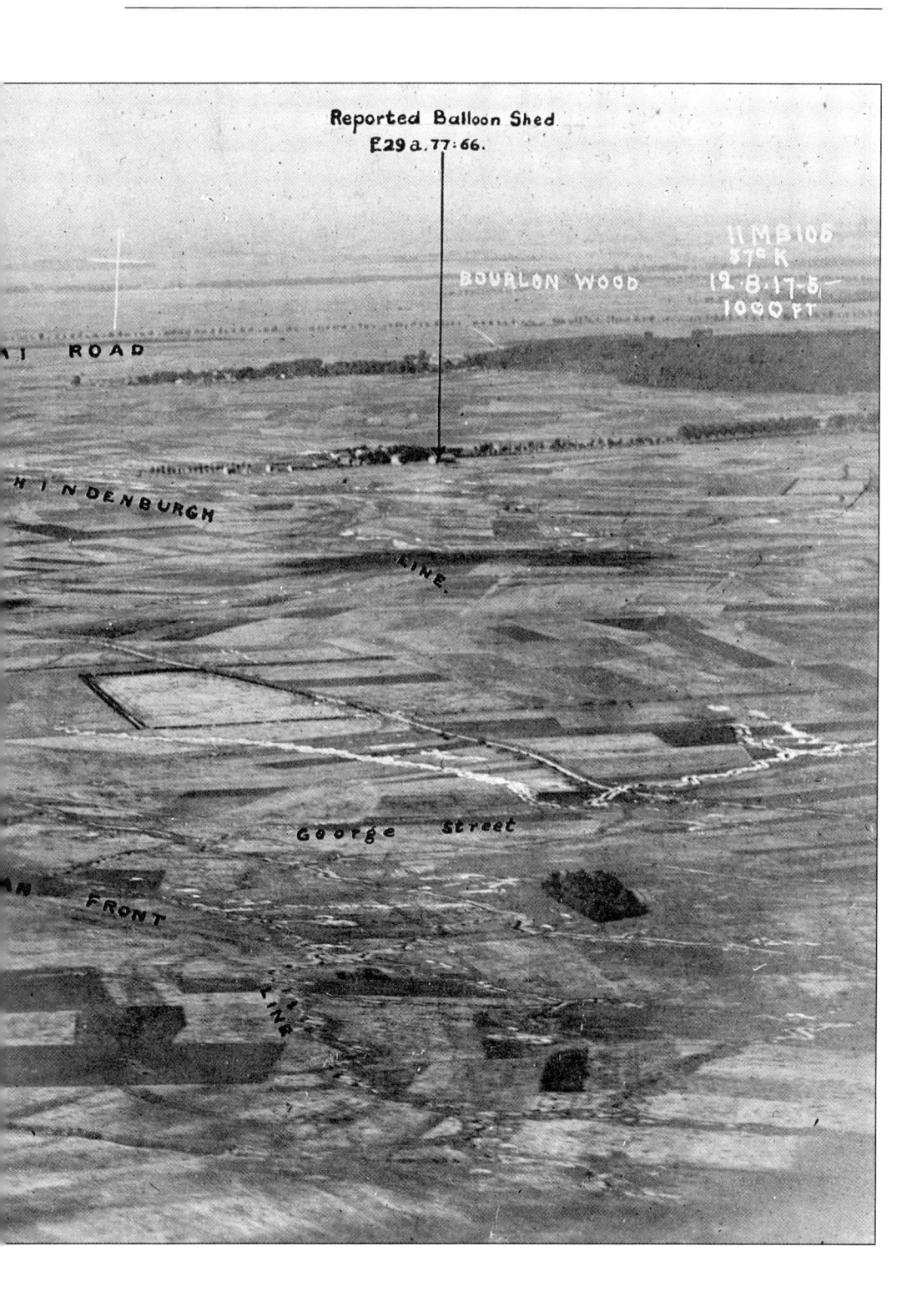

CAMBRAI

Reported Balloon Shed.
E 29 a. 77:66.

BOURLON WOOD

11 MB 105
57° K
12·8·17-5
1000 FT

...I ROAD

HINDENBURGH

LINE

George Street

...N FRONT

LINE

On 15 October the battalion was ordered to move to Auchy-les-Hesdin and hand over the camp to I Battalion. With the exception of the train, which was to take away the supply tanks, crashing into the ramp at Beaumetz, the move to Auchy was made without incident. The crews by this time were accustomed to the business of entraining, and it made little difference whether it was by night or day. Moreover, the men had become accustomed to making themselves comfortable at night in the train. At Erin the supply tanks were handed in, but the fighting tanks trekked to the old tankodrome at Auchy.

At this time the formation of the sections and companies was altered. Instead of three fighting sections, each of four tanks, and one supply section to each company, there were four fighting sections, each of three tanks, the question of supplies being under battalion arrangements. A fresh idea in the training of tanks was introduced when six tanks were sent to Eclimeux to train with the 12th Division and to clear passages through barbed wire by dragging grappling irons and steel cables.

During this period the battalion also made the acquaintance of the famous fascine. Officers from Central Workshops came round to the tankodrome to

Tanks, with their fascines in place, climb over an improvised ramp onto a train at the Plateau railhead. Notice how their sponsons have been folded in to clear lineside obstacles.

instruct the crews in the art of hoisting the huge bundles of brushwood without getting them crushed or damaged. The idea of this contrivance was to give the tail of the tank some support when crossing extra-wide trenches such as were supposed to exist along the Hindenburg Line.

On 13 November, 18th Company made the first move, trekking from Auchy to Erin ready for entraining for its unknown destination. On the 14th, both 16th and 17th Companies trekked to Erin and the whole three companies entrained on three trains the same day. That night, about 8 p.m., the train conveying 18th Company met with an accident at the horseshoe bend in the line between Bray-sur-Somme and Le Plateau junction. One of the trucks carrying the majority of the men of No. 12 Section jumped the rails at the head of the bend and, after jolting along for some time, overturned, shooting the men under the other wagons and causing several casualties. Sgt Sutton and Cpl Hicks were killed and eight other ranks injured.

Next day found the whole battalion assembled at Le Plateau, each in its own train. The day was spent in getting ammunition and stores aboard the trains and getting the fascines, which had been put on trucks at Central Workshops, into

A general view of the Plateau railhead, with three tank trains in steam and the 'gents' in the foreground.

position for conveying on top of the cab. As soon as it was dusk the trains left for the various detraining points. F Battalion detrained at Hendicourt and the spare tanks of the battalion at Sorrel.

The first stage of the approach march was from Hendicourt to Gouzeaucourt, while the spare tanks went to Dessart Wood where the crews continued to work on them. The three companies of fighting tanks arrived at Gouzeaucourt about an hour before dawn, and straightaway commenced camouflaging themselves under the ruins, which were all the Germans had left of this village. Gouzeaucourt, before the enemy retreat in the spring of 1917, was a village of considerable size with a number of shops, but in November 1917 it was nothing but ruins; indeed it was impossible to find a house which would serve as a billet. The strictest precautions were taken against discovery. No one was allowed to prowl about during the daytime and the camouflage of the tanks was kept intact until dusk, when the work of fixing spuds and getting the fascines into battle position began. At night no fires or lights were allowed.

During the next two days reconnaissance was made to the front line and the final preparations for action completed. On the afternoon of 19 November the CO, Col. Summers, visited the three companies and gave a short outline of the

The 6th Battalion tank *Firespite II* training in a ruined village.

scheme and plan of operations. Maps were given out and the CO wished everyone the best of luck. Just before this the Special Order of the Day, by Gen. Elles, calling on the Tank Corps for their best efforts, was issued. As soon as darkness permitted, the ROs taped the last stages of the approach march and marked each tank's position at the jumping-off point.

At about 9 p.m. on Monday night, 19 November, the battalion moved out of the various hiding places and commenced the final approach march. All the companies were in position by 3 a.m., and were soon joined by the infantry, who had to go over the top with them.

In this action the unicorn formation was adopted for the first time. Each section of three tanks was formed up in an equilateral triangle, the apex pointing towards the objective. The two rear tanks, each taking over with them a platoon of infantry who followed at a safe distance in snake formation.

About an hour before starting, rum was sent round, and each man was given a small tot to warm him, as the cold of the early morning was intense. The company commanders visited their tanks just before zero and wished everybody good luck and assured them it was going to be a walkover. The tanks cranked up engines at 5 a.m., and at 6.10 a.m. started to cover the remaining distance to the front line, followed by the infantry. The barrage came down at 6.20.

E BATTALION, 20 NOVEMBER 1917

Our particular mission, as the centre tank of a group of three, was to make for a particular piece of trench, drop our fascine and get over, the other two tanks of the group crossing in the same place. We crossed the narrow outpost line, got to our portion of the trench but found no Huns, they had retired, leaving their machine guns behind, but my gunners had a little practice potting at them. The Hindenburg Line was a truly formidable obstacle and we naturally had a few exciting moments. First, poised over the deep and wide excavation; then, releasing the fascine – would it drop alright? – we saw it lumber beautifully to the bottom. But could we get over? One can imagine our doubts as we had witnessed a few ghastly failures at Wailly. Anyhow, down we dropped and up, up, up – no one thought of the balance point – until at last we crashed upon the other side, splitting open my section commander's head and petrol cans, oil cans and ammunition boxes scattered all over the place. However, we had done the first part of our job successfully, and then the real fun began. The Hun was bravely standing on the fire step of his reserve trench, fully exposed and giving us rather a warm time with machine-gun and rifle fire. The first system was very quickly overcome and the battle developed into a tank race for the second system. The much-feared Grand Ravine was taken in third gear.

Our second objective was Flesquieres Chateau. Here stiff resistance was met; so well did the enemy resist that it was not cleared until the following morning. Our alignment and positions had been lost by this time, which led to individual attacks on various strongpoints. My particular tank, being a male, plugged the chateau and machine-gun emplacements in the vicinity for about ten minutes but, as there was no enemy in sight, I decided to get around to the rear of the chateau. Shells were dropping rather too near just now, which hastened our efforts. After crossing a deep sunken road, in which was one of our tank commanders repairing a broken track, we were asked by the infantry to clear a trench that was holding up their advance. The trench in question was on the reverse slope of Flesquieres Ridge, and therefore out of our sight. On gaining the crest of the ridge we seemed to walk right into it. Tanks were all over the place; some with noses up, some afire, but all motionless. At the time we hardly realized what had happened, however we spotted the offending trench, packed with Huns, fully exposed, and all their fire seemed concentrated on our tank. The trench was protected by a belt of wire about 50 yards deep. My gunners, in spite of the enemy's fire, were getting well on to their targets and I could observe the six pounder shells bursting on the parapet. About 20 yards into the

Tanks of 5th (E) Battalion knocked out on Flesquieres Ridge, with British soldiers in the deep German trenches.

German wire we received a direct hit which left a gaping hole in the side of the tank and wounded everyone except the driver and myself, but fortunately left the engine still running. As my gunners were out of action, and another shell landed amongst the sprockets, I ordered my driver to reverse out of the wire. We just reached the fringe when the engine petered out. A hasty examination showed the carburettor pierced by a splinter. Meanwhile a fire started on top of the tank, among some spare ammunition we were carrying. There was nothing left but to evacuate, which we did one by one, carrying the badly wounded back to our infantry. This left the driver and myself free to wend our way back to the battalion rallying point and observe how things were going. The Hun appeared to have wakened from his slumbers by this time, for his planes were flying very low and firing on our troops (one of them in fact was brought down by a gunner of the 5th Battalion) and the advance, in our sector at any rate, was held up. About noon a drizzle set in, and not having enough tanks left for a further attack it was decided to wait until dawn for a further effort. Being tankless we were ordered back to Havrincourt Wood and, although tired, hungry and very depressed at losing our tank, the sight of all the ground that had been gained with so little bloodshed, and the complete success of the surprise attack, acted upon us like a tonic. All troops seemed very pleased with the tanks; so pleased in fact that, I regret to mention, many were the drinks we had on the way back. It is really astonishing how much whisky the British Army carries into battle.

H BATTALION, 20 NOVEMBER 1917

I was a section commander with 8th (H) Battalion, Tank Corps when the Battle of Cambrai was fought, and as such had charge of three tanks, *Hadrian*, *Havoc* and *Hermosa*. They'd been concealed, with a number of others, in a small wood which we'd christened Horseshoe Wood because it was strewn with hundreds of these emblems of good luck. We moved up further during the night, to take our place ready for starting, and then we tried to snatch a little sleep inside the tanks. At an early hour sausages were sizzling on a Primus stove on the platform behind the engine, and mugs of hot tea were handed round.

Just before half-past six the barrage commenced, the guns reverberated like incessant thunder claps, and we started off. Our first bump came fairly soon. We climbed a bank, crashed through the hedge on top and came down heavily on the other side. Our tank weighed some 28 tons. When it lurched it threw its crew about like so many peanuts, and they had to clutch on to whatever they could when we were going over uneven ground. The perfect tank driver would balance his tank on the top of an ascent and let it down gently at just the right moment. But even perfect drivers got excited, and it was a good thing that tanks then had a maximum speed of only three miles an hour. When we'd crossed the front-line trenches our infantry followed us. The enemy had been taken completely by surprise and the sky in front was lit by his coloured SOS lights. It was a weird but impressive sight. The whole corps of 350 tanks was taking part and we were right in the centre of the battle line. On either side of us, as far as the eye could see, monstrous tanks, like prehistoric animals, each carrying an enormous bundle on its head, were advancing relentlessly. These bundles were called fascines, and could be dropped automatically to fill up the enemy trenches so that the tanks could cross without being ditched. Ahead of us, the General himself, with his head and shoulders sticking out of the top manhole of his flag tank *Hilda*, led the attack.

A section commander's job was to be where he could be of most use to the infantry, while still keeping control of his tanks. At Cambrai I went into action

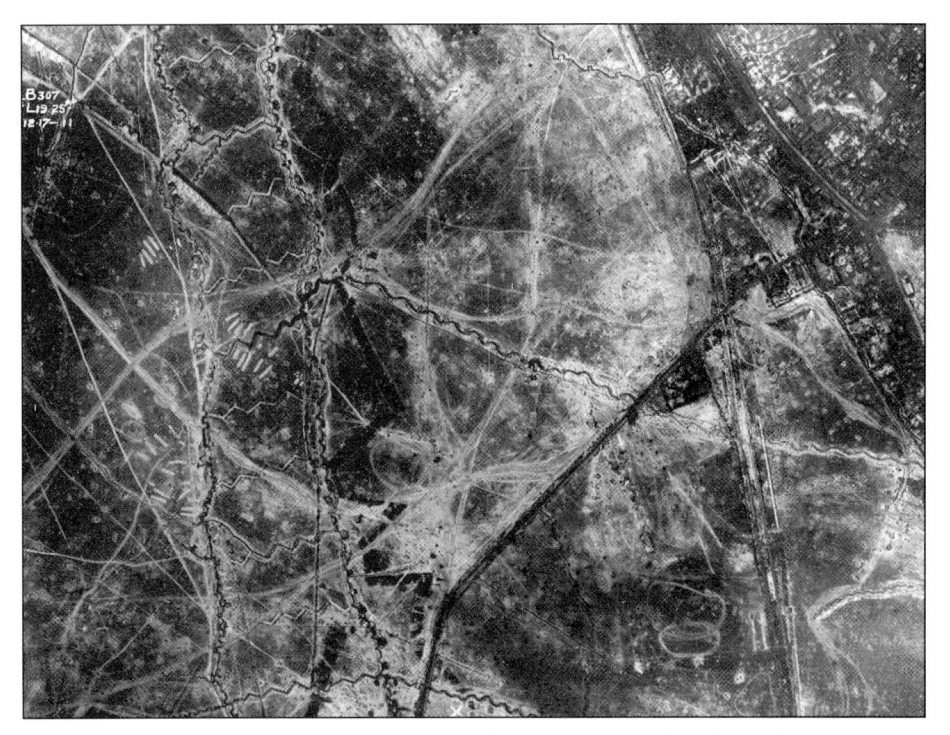

A vertical view of Flesquieres Ridge taken a month after the battle. The village of Ribecourt is at the bottom of the picture, with a mass of trenches in the centre. On the original print one can identify two German gun positions near the top of the picture, and at least five knocked-out tanks have been spotted. Most of the marks on the ground were made by tanks during the battle.

in *Hadrian* but there were times when I walked outside. The noise inside *Hadrian* was deafening; it almost drowned the noise of the barrage, and speech was practically impossible. I was in the left way to keep in touch with the tank commander. The shells from a single enemy gun were whizzing past us and falling among the infantry. Then machine-gun bullets began to rain on us; they sounded like the tapping of innumerable small hammers on *Hadrian's* sides. We clattered across no-man's land, crushing a path for the infantry through 50 yards of dense barbed wire. Then we crossed the main and reserve trenches of the Hindenburg Line – according to plan. The fascines were a great success. There was a congestion of traffic on the road outside Ribecourt and we had to take our turn in the queue of tanks waiting to enter the village. We'd been told to attack a particular piece of ground, but we found it deserted, so we sent off a carrier pigeon with news that we'd gained our objective.

Encouraged by our success we clattered across the fields in the direction of a neighbouring village. Just over half way there we came across a farmhouse with a nest of machine guns concealed in it. The tanks bombarded it and the enemy scattered. The three tanks now separated to clear the neighbourhood. About 11 o'clock I gave the return signal. I walked outside *Hadrian* and was surprised to see *Havoc's* commander escorting a bunch of prisoners at the point of his revolver. Single bullets swished past me and I noticed that each time *Havoc's* commander and his prize made a simultaneous genuflexion. The farm still contained a sniper; he was later disposed of. By 1 o'clock my section was back at the company rallying point. On our way we had the unpleasant experience of being shelled by a single field gun. Fortunately the shells went high and we escaped a direct hit by taking cover in a fold in the ground. A low-flying aeroplane was evidently hit by accident and fell in flames some little distance away.

Next morning we were told to move up to the Beetroot Factory at Flesquieres to get fresh orders. On our way we saw a number of tanks which had been knocked out the day before as they topped the Flesquieres ridge. They lay there in the form of a crescent – sixteen of them – with enormous gaping holes blown in their sides and fronts. One or two were a shapeless mass of steel.

At the Beetroot Factory we got our orders. We had to attack the village of Fontaine-Notre-Dame, just this side of Cambrai, and hold it until the infantry took over. There was another ridge to be crossed before we reached Fontaine, and since we'd already seen the mess that one enemy gun had made of tanks as they topped a ridge we didn't feel too comfortable about it – especially as the enemy was now prepared for tanks. At half past one seven tanks were drawn up in a line, at about 200 yard intervals, as though for a race. It was a clear, cold winter afternoon when we went into action for the second time in 48 hours.

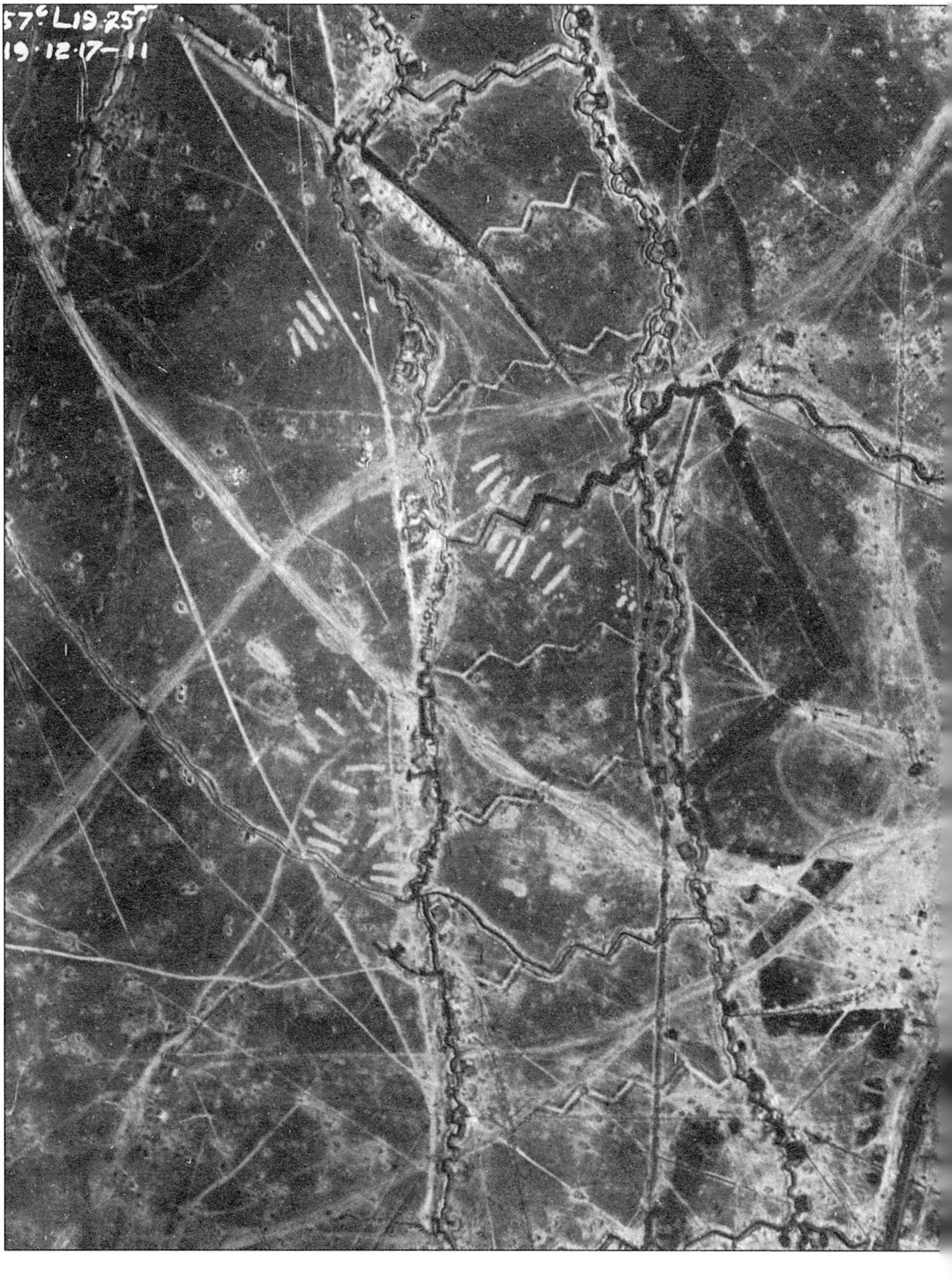
57c L19.25
19.12.17–11

CAMBRAI

The Mark IV male tank *Ernest* of E Battalion pauses while a wounded crew member is lifted into a Ford T ambulance during a lull in the battle.

The first half hour was uneventful and we rolled on comfortably over firm, smooth ground, Before we reached the ridge we had an encounter with the enemy at a village on the way. Our infantry had been forced to leave it, and we helped them to retake it. This delayed us half an hour. We then saw a tank of another battalion which had been knocked out a few hours earlier and was still blazing furiously. Evidently there was artillery on the other side of the ridge. When we reached the top of it we found ourselves in the thick of a bombardment. Two enemy batteries of field guns were blazing at the advancing tanks. *Hermosa* had taken a more direct route to Fontaine and was out of sight. One of the crew at the rear reported that *Havoc* was following, but that *Hydra* and *Harlequin* were knocked out.

All I could see through a revolver loophole was *Hong Kong* slightly ahead and about 200 yards to our left. She was coming in for the fury of the guns. Breathless we watched her zig-zag as the shells dropped nearer and nearer. Clouds of earth flew up like waterspouts – some so close that a dozen times we thought she'd been hit. For the moment we were safe, but we realized that whether she got through or not, in a minute or so we should be going through

Taken a week or so after the Battle of Cambrai, three wrecked F Battalion tanks are seen in the German wire.

the same hell. *Hadrian's* commander gave orders to keep on changing direction. Miraculously *Hong Kong* escaped and charged down the slope into the valley. Now it was our turn. Shells were bursting all round us and the fragments of them were striking the sides of the tank. Each of our six pounders required a gun layer and a gun loader, and while these four men blazed away, the rest of the perspiring crew kept the tank zig-zagging to upset the enemy's aim. It was a hard job to turn one of these early tanks. It needed four of the crew to work the levers, and they took their orders by signals. First of all the tank had to stop. A knock on the right side would attract the attention of the right gearsman. The driver would hold out a clenched fist, which was the signal to put the track into neutral. The gearsman would repeat the signal to show it was done. The officer, who controlled two brake levers, would pull on the right one, which held the right track. The driver would accelerate and the tank would slew round slowly on the stationary right track while the left track went into motion. As soon as the tank had turned sufficiently the procedure was reversed. Zig-zagging was, therefore, a slow and complicated business.

In between pulls on his brakes the tank commander fired the front machine gun. Our only hope of salvation was to keep going and to follow as erratic a

Tanks of 6 Company, E Battalion, lying abandoned on Flesquieres Ridge. The machine on the right, marked WC, is a wire-cutter.

course as possible. Just at this critical moment the Autovac, supplying petrol to the engine, failed. The engine spluttered and stopped. We were now a stationary target, incapable of moving one way or another. In the sudden silence we could hear the thud of falling shells, and metal and earth striking the sides of the tank. Any moment it would be Kingdom Come. The atmosphere in the tank was foul. To the heat and smell of the engine were added cordite fumes and the fact that nine men had been confined in this small space for close on three hours. It was a trying moment. With tense faces the crew watched the imperturbable second driver as he coolly and methodically put the Autovac right, ignoring all the proffered advice to give it a good hard knock and adjurations to 'hurry up or the bleeding tank would be blown to blazes'.

Across the valley, set serenely on a slight rise, was Fontaine-Notre-Dame with its peaceful roofs and spire silhouetted against the evening sky. It must have been only a matter of minutes before we got started again, but it seemed a life time. How we weren't hit during that brief period Providence alone knows. Then, down the slope we charged in top speed, with guns blazing, and the enemy batteries ceased firing.

Twilight was falling and there was a mist rising from the ground as we reached the outskirts of the village, which we scoured for half an hour without seeing

An oblique view of the battlefield, with the village of Anneux in the foreground and Fontaine-Notre-Dame on the main highway beyond. Marks left by the advancing tanks are visible everywhere.

any enemy. Cambrai was only two miles away – and the gate to it was ours. The tank commanders all told of shortage of petrol and ammunition; the male tanks had practically come to the end of their 200 rounds each of six-pounder shells; the engines of the tanks were running hot because of thin oil; and the crews were exhausted. If the infantry failed to turn up what orders should I give? The problem solved itself with the arrival of troops about half an hour later.

At about a quarter past five the three tanks *Hadrian*, *Havoc* and *Hong Kong*, lumbering along like circus elephants, one following the other, started back. Our compasses appeared not to be reading true so we took as a landmark a blazing object which we presumed was a tank still on fire. All went well until we got in among some trenches. In the darkness it was difficult for the tanks to progress without danger of being ditched, so *Havoc's* commander and I walked in front with flashlamps to explore the ground and pick out the best way. Coming upon a steep bank, which proved to be the side of a sunken

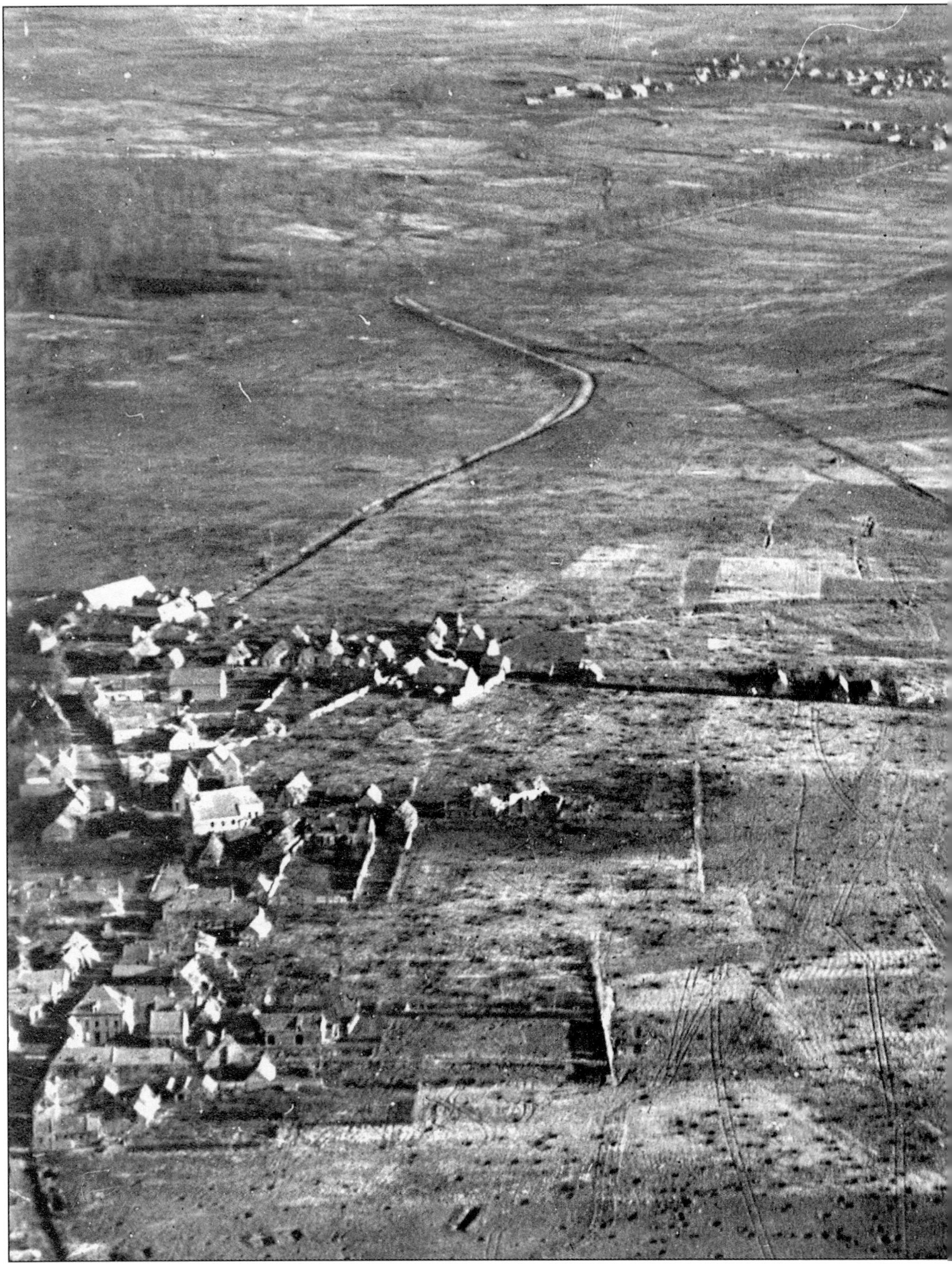

12 L.O. 31.
57° ANNEUX &
FONTAINE NOTRE DAME
2.12.17.10.

German troops with a knocked-out Mark IV female in Fontaine-Notre-Dame. Tanks proved very vulnerable when fighting in defended villages.

road, we stopped the tanks and explored along the top in the hope of finding a shallow place in which to cross; suddenly shadowy figures loomed up against the white of the road; we challenged them, drawing our revolvers, to learn that they were stretcher bearers of the 51st Division, collecting dead and wounded. They directed us. In a village through which we passed *Hadrian's* petrol ran out, and a leak was discovered in the radiator; the journey was completed on the iron ration of petrol and water. This village was the one we had helped the infantry to recapture during the afternoon. Now we found the 4th Battalion, The Gordon Highlanders in possession. I learned that their commanding officer was an old school fellow of mine from the Argentine, whom I had not seen for ten years. At the age of 25 he was a Lieutenant Colonel! The Jocks told us with pride that he had ridden in on horseback at the head of his battalion when they entered to take possession of the village. I was conducted to him and he remarked on the day's success, saying that the tanks had proved their worth.

Nearing our rallying point I met the second-in-command of our company walking in the direction of Fontaine. He had come out to look for us, to tell us

A female tank moving up to attack Bourlon Wood on the 23rd passes captured German guns near Graincourt.

to return, in case we had intended spending the whole night there. He took me to the tank company commander, to whom I reported the capture of the objective. When we had parked the tanks, after our return, the crews were deaf from the infernal noise, and were sick when they got out into the clean, fresh air after almost eleven hours in the foul atmosphere of the tanks.

Hermosa turned up, and reported a most eventful day. She had reached Fontaine about four o'clock – about the time we encountered the bombardment on the ridge. In front of Fontaine she had had her left front machine gun put out of action by a shell and one man had been slightly wounded. The gun was so smashed that it could not be replaced, having become jammed in the turret. She had entered the village, reconnoitred most of its streets, and had even proceeded a little way along the road to Cambrai, with the enemy retiring in front of her. In the village, on seeing a light in a house, her commander, accompanied by his corporal, entered and found that it was inhabited by French civilians; two Frenchmen, in their delight, embraced and kissed the corporal while an old lady brought out her purse and offered money to the commander who, of course, refused it, but accepted a cup of coffee instead. After patrolling

A victorious female tank of 3rd (C) Battalion, flying her battalion colours, drags a captured German 5.9 in. gun into a wood near Ribecourt.

the streets for about an hour, waiting for the infantry, he saw figures approaching in the darkness and shouted 'Halt! Who are you? Are you English?' 'No' came the emphatic reply 'we're Scottish.' They were Argyll and Sutherland Highlanders of the 51st Division who had entered to take over. *Hermosa* had not left till five fifty, but in the darkness we had missed her.

The total advance in the two days had been about seven miles, and our capture of Fontaine-Notre-Dame was the culminating point of the advance on Cambrai. It was lost next day and never wholly retaken, in spite of heavy fighting.

CHAPTER FIVE

Villers-Bretonneux

The events of March and April 1918 were dominated by a strong German attack against Allied positions, notably in the Somme valley. The Revolution in Russia had relieved pressure on their eastern front, enabling the Germans to move large forces to the west, but they had also adopted new tactics of infiltration, seeking weak points in the Allied line. They also started to use tanks for the first time.

For the British it was a time of improvization; developing defensive tactics for tanks and converting many crews into Lewis gun teams in order to hold the line. There were two significant events from the tank point of view which occurred within a short time and in sight of each other. One was the very first tank versus tank action, when British and German machines exchanged shots for the first time. The other was a more one-sided encounter when six of the new British Whippet tanks got in among two German infantry battalions and decimated them. However, as the following German account shows, they did not escape unscathed.

The German A7V tank, conceived as a response to the British initiative, was hastily designed but technically advanced. Weighing 30 tons and armed with one 57 mm gun and six Maxim machine guns, it was more in the style of a travelling fortress, lacking the cross-country mobility of the British tanks. It required a crew of eighteen and was powered by twin Daimler engines, driving through a sophisticated gearbox. Accorded a low priority for production, only twenty were completed when the war ended, but Villers-Bretonneux marked their debut and their greatest success.

The Whippet tank was designed in 1917 by William Tritton of Fosters. As its name implies, it was designed as a fast pursuit tank to exploit any breakthrough achieved by the heavy machines. It had a top speed of about 8 m.p.h. and was powered by two 45 h.p. Tylor engines, each with its own clutch and gearbox. It was always difficult to drive but in skilled hands proved very effective. It weighed 14 tons, had a crew of three and mounted three Hotchkiss machine guns.

1ST TANK BATTALION, MARCH 1918

While trekking from Tincourt Station to Buire Wood one tank, No. 2048 under 2nd Lt. Dudley broke down 1½ miles from the latter place and it was

Tanks on a trek, awaiting orders near Mont St Eloi on 4 April 1918.

found necessary to remove the engine. On the morning of the 21st at 4.40 a.m. the enemy commenced that heavy bombardment which was to prelude a period of the most strenuous activity and nerve shaking anxiety which has ever been experienced by the British Army. During the following fortnight the battalion was engaged in a continuous rearguard action, during which it formed, at more than one time, the rearguard of the army.

At 9 a.m. the enemy launched his infantry attack and all the tanks of the battalion were filled up ready for action. At 6 a.m. on the 22nd orders were received by telephone from the 4th Brigade to man battle positions, and all ranks at once proceeded to the tankodrome. At 9 a.m. orders were received that all tanks were to be moved from Buire Wood to Three Tubs Wood and by 10 a.m they were all *en route*, with the exception of No. 2048 which was having its engine replaced. Lt Dudley was ordered to destroy the tank if there was any likelihood of its falling into the hands of the enemy. Up till this time the seriousness of the position had not been generally realized, and it was thought that there would be a counter attack immediately which would throw the enemy back to his previous position and beyond. We had yet to learn that this was no mere spasmodic raid, but an action commenced with reasonable certainty of success after long months of scheming and preparation. The enemy attack continued, and owing to the proximity of the enemy infantry Lt Dudley blew up his tank and rejoined his battalion along with his crew.

At 11 a.m. verbal orders were received from 4th Tank Brigade Intelligence Officer that the battalion was to move immediately to Moislains. No transport was available until 2 p.m., when two lorries reported. Considerable mechanical trouble was experienced during the journey to Moislains but all tanks arrived eventually. The night of the 22nd was spent in a position just west of Moislains, and at 6 a.m. on the 23rd our infantry received orders to retire, and the battalion took up position on the high ground north-west of Moislains. A and B Companies lined the ridge at 50 pace intervals and C Company were held in reserve. Before this position was reached two tanks had to be destroyed. These were destroyed, as was a petrol dump which seemed to be in danger of capture. One supply tank was evacuated from Moislains less than half an hour before the village was captured, and the fighting tank under 2/Lt MacFayden developed mechanical trouble and was destroyed. This officer and his crew stayed by the tank and with their Lewis guns inflicted enormous losses on the advancing enemy, even capturing several of the most venturesome.

It was now realized that the enemy was outflanking us in the direction of Bouchavesnes, and consequently orders were issued to withdraw to the ridge north of Clery-sur-Somme. A position was taken up there behind a strong belt of wire and an outpost from each section was sent out in front. In addition two complete sections were detailed as outposts. At 1 a.m. on the 24th orders were received to withdraw to a line east of Haricourt. A considerable number of tanks were unable to complete this journey and were consequently destroyed. That afternoon at 2 p.m. two sections were sent forward, one under Capt Dorman, in a south-easterly direction towards Hem; the other, under Capt Fraser, in a north-easterly direction to Mauripas. These two sections fought an action during the afternoon and evening, and what remained of them returned to Mericourt at midnight. Another notable action was fought on the same day by Lt Oldham, who held out alone at Curlu for 24 hours. By midnight Maj. Thorpe had established a line of Lewis-gun posts in the trenches 700 yards east of Mericourt, and the remainder of the battalion withdrew to a position north-east of Bray, where it rested for three hours. On the morning of the 25th at 4 a.m. orders were received to take a position in the Bois de Tailles, and while in this position the tanks were made fit for fighting. At 4 p.m. Maj. Thorpe rejoined the battalion with the Lewis-gun crews which had been holding the line in front of Mericourt, and Capt Keogh moved forward to Méaulte with nine tanks to engage the enemy who were attacking fiercely in that sector. On the 26th the enemy attacked heavily, and for four hours were

Although this photo shows Canadian troops near Bony in June 1918, it serves to show a typical Lewis-gun team, viewed from the cab of a tank, as they dig in at a roadside ditch.

held in check by the gun teams who succeeded in inflicting heavy casualties on the attacking infantry. During this attack the gun teams were absolutely without any support of any kind. A very fine example was set by one gun team consisting of Capt Sunnikin, Lt Ehrhardt and Sgt Scott whose success was nothing short of miraculous as they were hemmed in on three sides by the enemy.

Under cover of this rearguard action all the supply tanks were withdrawn to Heilly, where a suitable bridge across the Ancre was found. Sections of the battalion crossed the Ancre at various places and the battalion finally rallied at Franvillers on the 27th. On the 28th ground was reconnoitered for Lewis-gun posts on the ridge south of Brizieux. These posts were occupied in conjunction with the Australian infantry and in the afternoon a section of C Company proceeded to Mericourt and took up a position in the valley behind the village. One tank from C Company was sent to Bonnay and attached to the Australians. The 28th, 29th and 30th were spent in reorganizing the battalion into Lewis-gun teams and bringing the remaining tanks into fighting condition.

The month concluded with Easter Sunday, on which a church service was held. The enemy was brought to a standstill on the Morlancourt to Villers-

A Mark IV female seen in Peronne, 23 March 1918.

Bretonneux line and was thereafter unable to make any progress in that sector. During the withdrawal the condition of the villagers was pitiful. Women and children and old men, crazed with fright and with the liveliest memories of the conduct of the Germans in the area occupied by them, were to be seen streaming westwards from their homes, pushing their meagre possessions before them in handcarts and alternately invoking the aid of their saints and calling down their wrath upon the hated Boche.

1ST BATTALION, APRIL 1918

On 1 April C Company took over all the fighting tanks in the battalion, while A and B Companies were formed into Lewis-gun teams ready to proceed to the forward area that they might assist in the event of an enemy attack. In order that these companies might be moved rapidly in the case of necessity, five 3 ton lorries were placed at the disposal of the battalion. On the 2nd, 3rd and 4th, A and B Companies carried out machine-gun training while C Company were engaged in preparing their tanks for action. On the 5th, B Company sent a party

French artillery passing British troops and tanks in Aveluy, 25 March 1918.

to Beauval to draw ten Mark IV tanks, their example being followed by A Company who drew twelve Mark IV tanks from Vighacourt on the 6th. The following day the battalion and company headquarters moved from Franvillers to Behencourt, where orders were received from the 4th Brigade that the battalion would no longer act as reserve Lewis-gun teams, its place being taken by 4th Battalion. All company headquarters moved on the following day. On the 9th battalion headquarters also moved, going from Behencourt to Frechencourt. While the tanks were lying up in a wood, orders were received that all sprockets were to be changed and when this was completed two sections of A Company moved to Bois d'Aquenne and Bois de Blangy, while company headquarters was established in a small wood nearby. On the 12th, the battalion was attached to the 3rd Brigade and on the following day the other two sections of A Company moved up. On the 15th and 16th, A and B Companies prepared their tanks for action, the distinguishing marks for aeroplanes being painted for the first time. This mark consisted of three stripes, white, red and white, painted on the roof of the cab.

On the 17th the Bois d'Aquenne was heavily shelled with mustard gas, which was used here for the first time. As a result of this bombardment six officers and 32 other ranks of A Company were evacuated to hospital, their places being

A horse-drawn Mark VI four-stretcher ambulance passing a knocked-out female tank on the edge of the battlefield. The tank displays the red/white/red markings adopted at this time.

filled by reinforcements from the other two companies. The company was immediately moved to Bois d'Abbé to guard against a repetition of this bombardment. At this period the Bois d'Abbé presented a most picturesque spectacle and anyone taking the trouble to walk through it could have the unique experience of seeing practically every branch of both the British and French armies represented. In this wood were to be found tanks of all descriptions: Mark IVs, Whippets and French Renaults, heavy and light artillery, British infantry, Australians, French cavalry, infantry, Moroccans, and a detachment of the Legion of Frontiersmen mounted on little Arab ponies, which were a strange contrast to the heavy Percherons of the artillery.

On the 18th, Col. Broome fell sick and had to go to hospital, and Maj. Tilly again assumed command of the Battalion. On the following day an extensive reconnaissance was carried out of lying-up points, etc. which could be used in the event of an enemy attack. This proved to be a very necessary precaution, for at 3.30 a.m. on the 24th a very heavy enemy barrage was put down north and south of the Somme, followed by a strong infantry attack at 6 a.m. in the Villers-Bretonneux area. Assistance from the tanks was asked for and A Company was sent to cooperate with the 3rd Corps.

At 8.30 a.m. No. 1 Section, under Capt J.C. Brown MC, moved forward and engaged the enemy at Cachy, where it was attacking strongly with the aid of three tanks. Capt Brown's tanks at once engaged these, but both his females received direct hits from the gun which the Germans were carrying and had to fall out of action. This left Lt Mitchell alone in command of a male tank. He immediately engaged the three enemy tanks and at 10.15 obtained a direct hit on the leader. This he followed with two more hits in quick succession on the same tank, putting it out of action. On seeing the fate of their leader and realizing that the British tank was turning its attention to them, the remaining German tanks thought discretion the better part of valour and fled, leaving Lt Mitchell the master of the situation. This action is particularly interesting to the Tank Corps for this was the first occasion on which tank met tank, and the complete victory of the British reflects great credit on Capt Brown's section for inflicting ignominious defeat on the tanks with which the enemy had hoped to crush the British opposition and take Amiens.

At 1 p.m. Capt Groves' section went into action by the railway, followed by Lt Holton's section, which threw back in disorder strong detachments of the enemy, who had succeeded in penetrating Allied defences as far as the outskirts of the Bois d'Aquenne. This concluded the enemy attack in this sector and it is an indisputable fact that, had it not been for the magnificent part played by this company in the battle, the enemy would have broken through and would probably have succeeded in cutting the Amiens-Abbeville railway, a disaster which would have had an incalculable effect on subsequent operations.

Two days later fighting was resumed, A Company being reinforced by a section of C Company under Capt Hunnikin MC. The attack was carried out by the Moroccan Division, which included in its ranks the famous Foreign Legion, and the first wave went over at 5.30 a.m. At 6 a.m. the enemy launched a counterattack, being greatly assisted by a heavy mist which hid its advancing infantry. Capt Groves' section, however, got in among the Germans and caused them enormous casualties. The French infantry then rallied and the attack was brought to a standstill. A noteworthy part was played in the action by 2/Lt Wilson, who broke through the enemy's line and advanced right through Villers-Bretonneux. During this action Lt Wilson found himself among some German heavy guns, which he attacked with case shot and machine-gun fire, killing most of their personnel and dispersing the rest. He then patrolled some trenches manned by the enemy and caused them some enormous losses by his enfilade fire. Eventually, having fired every round of ammunition in his tank, he decided to return, but while on his way back his magneto broke down and could not be repaired. Lt Wilson therefore sent a messenger back to obtain a new magneto and after this had been fitted he rejoined the battalion with the disproportionate casualties of two men slightly wounded.

After this action an inter-company relief was carried out, C Company taking over A Company's tanks south of the Somme and A Company returning to Franvillers Wood. On the following day orders were received for four tanks to cooperate with the Moroccan Division in an attack which was to take place on the 28th on Mangard Wood. Owing to a mistake on the part of the French guides, the four tanks did not get into action but 2/Lt Jones left his tank and got in touch with a detachment of French infantry who assisted him in locating his objectives, which were situated in the wood. He then returned to his tank and took it into action, clearing numerous machine-gun nests and rendering valuable assistance to the infantry. This officer stayed in the wood until he had expended all his ammunition and then, as the infantry decided not to make a further attack, he withdrew and rejoined the company. Though wounded himself, he insisted upon evacuating his crew, who were all wounded, in the ration cart, before he would allow himself to be treated. He was then evacuated himself and his condition was sufficiently serious to warrant his removal to England. This action gained for Lt Jones the immediate award of the Military Cross.

3RD BATTALION, 24 APRIL 1918

This action was performed by what was known as X Company of the 3rd Battalion. This was an emergency Company formed from C Company to go and assist in the defence of Amiens. The Company consisted of seven Whippet tanks. I was in command, and the section commanders were Lts Hore and Elsbury.

At 10.30 a.m. on 24 April I was lying up in a small wood near the Bois de Blangy when I received orders from 58th Division to whom I was attached, giving the information that an aeroplane had just dropped a message to say that a force, estimated at about two enemy battalions, were massing for attack about 1,000 yards east of Cachy and ordering my company to disperse them before they could launch their attack. It was a cold morning, and our engines were already running to warm up, so we were off at once. I led the tanks until we reached a small hollow where I left them and rode forward to reconnoitre.

Here I was delighted to meet Capt Sheppard of the Northamptons (my own old regiment), then commanding what was known as Sheppard's Force. He informed me that the first phase of the enemy attack on our line had worn itself out, but that he was expecting a renewal at any moment, and indicating the region where he judged the leapfrogging troops must be assembling. I

Whippet tanks preparing for action near Albert on 28 March 1918. A crew member is handling a Hotchkiss machine gun at the rear door of the nearest tank.

Whippets and infantry moving forward near Mailly-Maillet in March 1918.

Another picture taken on 28 March shows Whippets on the move near Albert.

ascertained that the country was beautifully open and undulating, and ideal for tanks, and galloped back to the company.

    I assembled section and tank commanders quickly, gave them the information where I considered the two battalions to be, ordered them to form line, facing south at 50 paces interval between tanks, cross the Cachy Switch (no obstacle, battered to pieces) and charge at full speed southwards, dispersing any enemy met on the way. On reaching a sky line which I indicated, they were to turn back and charge through the enemy again on the way back. My deductions as to the position of the enemy proved correct. The charging tanks came upon them over a rise, at point-blank range, apparently having a meal as several bodies had laid aside arms. The tanks went straight through them, causing great execution by fire, and by running over many who were unable to get away. They turned and came back through the remnants again, utterly dispersing them, and the second phase of the attack on our line that day never materialized. We lost one tank, the tank commander in his enthusiasm crossing the sky line which I had indicated as the limit of advance, and being knocked out by a battery placed somewhere in the vicinity of Hangard Wood. What the total casualties of the enemy were is unknown, but 400 dead at any rate were counted later.

A painting of the action by X Company at Cachy. Sgt Parrott's tank, as described in Capt Price's report, is in the centre.

We started at 10.30 a.m. and were back again by 2.30 p.m. One misapprehension regarding the picture I should like to point out. The letter P on tank A277 is not, as is commonly supposed, my initial. It is the initial of the tank commander, Sgt Parrott, who commanded this tank with great gallantry in this and other actions.

Signed Capt T.R. Price, DSO MC

STURM PANZERKRAFTWAGEN ABTEILUNGEN 1, 2 AND 3, 24TH APRIL 1918

On the evening of 21 April a detachment of thirteen German tanks was detrained at Guillaucourt, where one, due to a cracked cylinder head, was left, and the remaining twelve moved to Wiencourt, their second line transport remaining at the detraining station. While they were being detrained they were bombed by aircraft but suffered no inconvenience, and neither did the hostile aircraft discover the nature of their target.

On the 22nd the detachment was organized into three groups and their leaders were given their instructions; the situation and objectives were explained. Contact was also obtained with the infantry to be supported by the tanks, and the plans and execution of the attack were discussed with them.

An oblique view of the battlefield, with Villers-Bretonneux in the left foreground.

Further, a munition and fuel depot was established at Guillaucourt. If the attack proved successful, each group was to be supplied by two lorries, one with ammunition and the other with petrol, which were to advance at first as far as Wiencourt, and later as far as Marcelcave. Any further advance of these supply lorries was to be left to the discretion of the group leaders.

On 23 April the tasks for Lt Scopnik's group (attached to 228th Infantry Division) and for Lt Uihlein's group (attached to 4th Guards Infantry Division) were outlined as follows:

1) The Scopnik group, after the penetration of Villers-Bretonneux by the infantry, was to support the advance north of this village, and to return to the rendezvous as soon as the 228th Infantry Division reached its first day's objective north of Villers-Bretonneux.

2) The Uihlein group was to support the advance of the infantry into Bois d'Aquenne after Villers-Bretonneux had been taken, and to return to the rendezvous after the infantry had penetrated the wood.

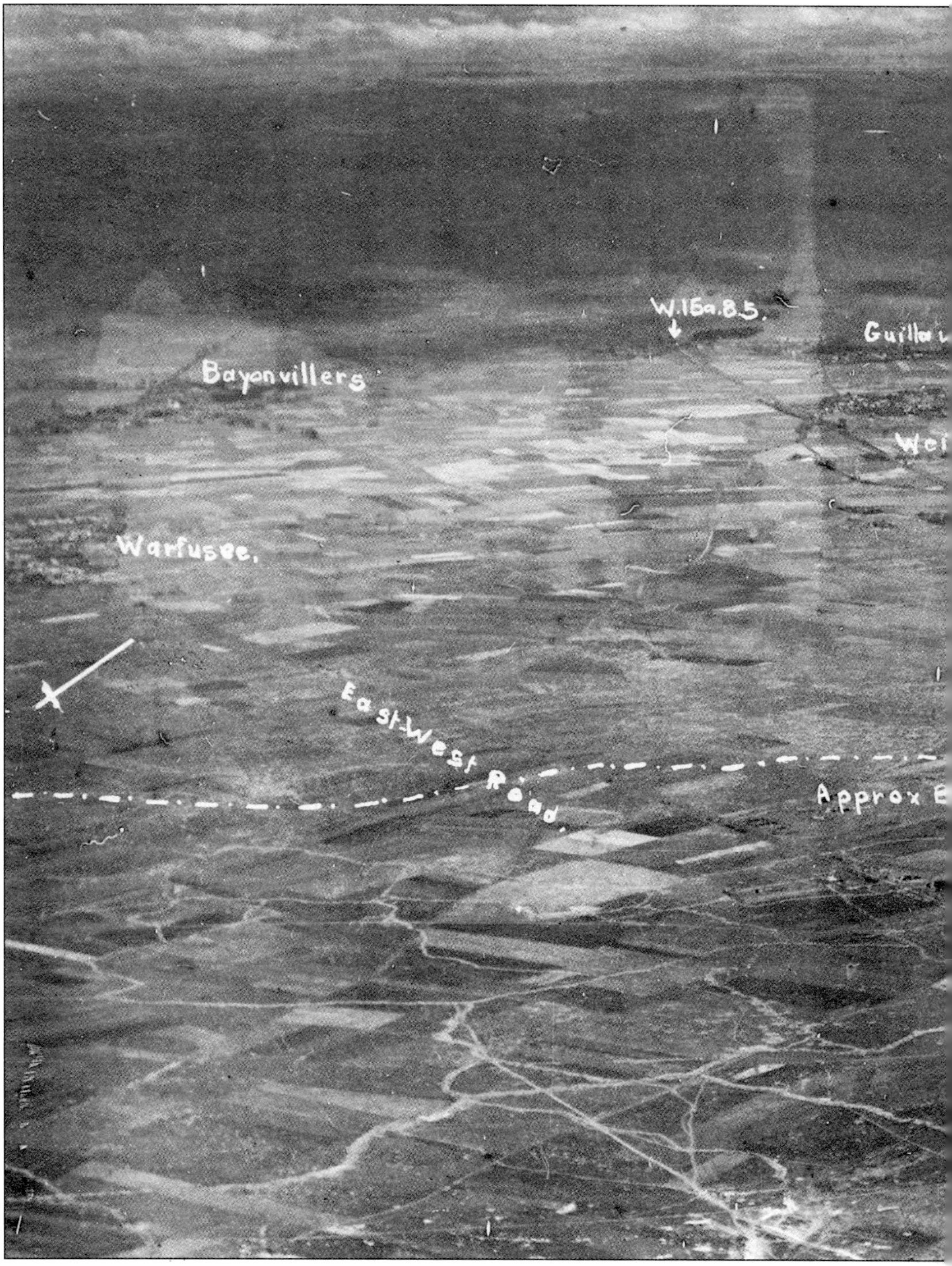
W.15a.8.5.
Guilla
Bayonvillers
Wei
Warfusee.
East-West Road
Approx E

VILLERS-BRETONNEUX

An A7V tank from Abteilung 2, with most of its crew riding on top, at a railhead.

Besides these orders, instructions were given to all groups to hold themselves ready to act on their own initiative in the case of enemy counterattacks.

At 4.45 a.m. on 24 April all the tanks began the advance to their starting lines, which were reached punctually. As these positions were close behind the German front line, they advanced after the preliminary bombardment opened, in order to prevent the enemy from hearing the noise of the engines.

The early stages of the attack took place in thick fog, which began to clear about 11 a.m. The condition of the ground was extremely favourable for the tanks, because the country to be traversed consisted mainly of dry cultivated land and grass, and was almost entirely free from obstacles such as trenches and shell holes.

The Scopnik group left its starting line at 6.50 a.m., crossed the German front line at 7 a.m., and the enemy front line shortly afterwards. The enemy front-line troops defended their position obstinately, the concealed machine-gun nests being difficult to recognize in the thick fog. A heavy fire was opened on the tanks. After a short but violent fight, the enemy infantry occupying the front-line trench and the garrisons of the machine-gun nests surrendered. The prisoners were driven into the arms of the German infantry who were following the tanks.

The crew of an A7V rest with their machine in Villers-Bretonneux. A camouflage net is draped over the driving cab.

Tank No. 3 (Oberleutnant Scopnik) proceeded under heavy enemy rifle and artillery fire parallel to the railway to within about 100 metres of the eastern outskirts of Villers-Bretonneux. As the infantry did not follow, and because by this time they had entirely lost touch with them, the tank proceeded to return, destroyed four machine-gun nests which had attacked it in the rear, and then accompanied the infantry, who by this time had caught it up, to the eastern outskirts of Villers-Bretonneux, close by the railway embankment. Here it came under heavy machine-gun fire. The tank then proceeded along the edge of Villers-Bretonneux and cleaned up the machine-gun nests in that quarter, in spite of an obstinate defence. It then pushed forward with the infantry into the village and proceeded as far as the railway crossing, close to the Roman road on the western outskirts. In the course of this manoeuvre considerable enemy resistance was broken. Tanks Nos 1 and 2 (Leutnants Vietze and Volkheim), in the course of their advance, succeeded in cleaning up strongly entrenched machine-gun nests which had been holding up the advance of the German infantry, and at 8.45 a.m., joined tank No. 3 in front of the brickworks. It was only then that visibility became good enough to enable touch to be kept between the three tanks.

The brickworks, which were strongly held by machine guns, were attacked by the three tanks together and paralysed by their fire. Those of the garrison who were still alive surrendered. The prisoners were driven towards the German infantry. While the infantry occupied the brickworks, tanks Nos 1 and 2 advanced on the hangars which were situated on the eastern outskirts of Villers-Bretonneux and which were defended by numerous machine-gun nests. The hangars were destroyed by fire. The tanks then proceeded along the eastern outskirts of the village and reached the Roman road, having silenced several machine guns placed in houses.

At midday the tanks returned to their starting-line position, having performed their allotted tasks. Losses: one officer severely wounded; two men killed; 15 men wounded (including four of the accompanying troops).

Shortly after 7 a.m. the Uihlein group crossed their own front line. Tanks Nos 1 and 2 (Leutnants Hennecke and Burmann) advanced along the railway embankment towards Villers-Bretonneux, attacked a well-fortified strongpoint in front and flank, and finally in the rear, causing the garrison to evacuate it and thus enable the infantry to advance. Tank No. 2 then cleared a trench running in a westerly direction as far as the chapel, and killed a number of the enemy and took thirteen prisoners. Then, in company with tank No. 1, it proceeded in a westerly direction through the railway station. Tank No. 2, in the course of this advance, successfully engaged a number of enemy reinforcements which had been hastily brought up, and at 10 a.m. reached the Roman road below the railway crossing. In the meantime, Tank No. 1, in spite of a defect in its gun mounting due to continual rolling and rocking, destroyed several strongpoints and joined Tank No. 2. Both tanks then opened a heavy fire in the Bois d'Aquenne and on the enemy reserves which had just arrived west of this wood, which the German infantry was thus enabled to enter. Tank No. 3 (Leutnant Theunissen) was only intended to deal with the enemy resistance in the early stages of the battle and then join Tanks Nos 1 and 2. It advanced, however, over the enemy front line and cleared the enemy trenches from the flank and rear, in the course of which operation thirty prisoners were taken. It then moved towards a fortified farm, the garden being reached before engine trouble set in. En route it had dealt with several machine-gun nests. In spite of a defective engine it succeeded in breaking down enemy resistance south of the railway station, where it captured one officer and 174 men. The tank was then put entirely out of action, owing to blockages in the valves and in the induction pipe. Leutnant Theunissen advanced with his men on foot, but as repairs were completed shortly afterwards, he returned to the tank. A few minutes later he ran into a shell hole, where the machine stuck and partially capsized. During the night two attempts were made to save the tank, but these proved unsuccessful. It was left lying in the farm near the German front line and was prepared for demolition. The gun and machine guns could not be saved on account of the suddenness and violence of the enemy's counterattacks, which the German infantry failed to repulse.

Tanks Nos 4 and 5 (Leutnants Block and Bartens) were to advance against the fortified farmhouse south of Villers-Bretonneux. Tank No. 6 (Leutnant Lappe) was to advance on the farm from the south, in order to support Tanks Nos 4 and 5 from the flank. Tank No. 4 reached the enemy front line at 7.10 a.m., cleared a section of trench, broke down the strong resistance offered at the farm and thus paved the way for the infantry. This tank then joined Tanks Nos 1 and 2, and advanced with them towards the Bois d'Aquenne. In conjunction with these two tanks, it was successful in repulsing an enemy counterattack.

Tank No. 5, on account of the thick fog, proceeded rather too far to the north, and was met by heavy machine-gun fire. The driver was wounded and the brakes jammed. Leutnant Bartens, together with all available members of the crew, joined the infantry, but a little later on, the repairs having been completed, he returned to the tank, which advanced on the hill in front of the Bois d'Aquenne, where it cleaned up a number of the enemy holding sections of a trench and some machine-gun nests.

Tank No. 6 (Leutnant Lappe) advanced in accordance with orders. The German infantry, however, did not follow. The tank was engaged in heavy enemy fire. At a distance of 30 metres in front of the enemy both engines became overheated and broke down. The driver was wounded and no second

The sinister shapes of *Hagen* and *Schnuck*, photographed in a smoke screen at Villers-Bretonneux.

driver was available because the three second drivers of the detachment were still being trained with the *Rohr Sturmabteilung*. After some time, however, Leutnant Lappe succeeded in starting the engines and then returned slowly to his original position. Losses: one man killed; two officers and 22 men wounded (including 13 of the accompanying infantry).

The Steinhart group (attached to the 77th Reserve Division) reached its starting line at 6.40 a.m.

Tank No. 1 (Leutnant Stein) advanced with the first infantry wave, silencing a number of machine guns and clearing up several sections of trench. At 9.45 a.m., however, the tank ran onto a patch of undermined ground, turned over on its right side and was thus out of action. The crew, under the orders of the commander, left the tank and took part in the infantry battle as *Sturmtruppen* with three machine guns. The tank was blown up by a pioneer officer when our infantry retired. It could not be saved on account of enemy counterattacks.

Tank No. 2 (Leutnant Biltz) advanced in the direction of Cachy and cleared up several machine-gun nests, including one which had held up a German infantry battalion for over an hour. The tank then advanced to within 700 metres of Cachy, effectively bombarding the enemy position there. Next it was

Leutnant Stein's tank *Elfriede*, which toppled over into a sandpit during the battle.

engaged by eight enemy tanks which suddenly appeared. It put out of action one of these machines and compelled another to retire. Almost immediately after this, however, it received a direct hit from the enemy artillery and the armour was pierced by a projectile of about 5.7 cm calibre. Another direct hit was made on the right front of the tank and a third was received in the oil tank. In spite of this, however, the tank was successfully brought back as far as the first infantry position, a distance of roughly two kilometres. It was so badly damaged that it was prepared for blowing up. No further efforts to save the tank could be made because shortly afterwards the enemy recaptured the ground taken.

Tank No. 3 (Leutnant Müller-Albert) was ordered to support the infantry attack in the direction of Gentelles. The attack in this sector, however, was soon held up. The tank, therefore, assisted tank No. 4 in attacking Cachy with gunfire on the eastern edge of the village. As the infantry did not assault Cachy, the tank returned to its rendezvous.

Tank No. 4 (Leutnant Bitter), in the course of its advance on Cachy, destroyed several machine-gun nests. The garrison of a trench about 200 metres long was attacked from the flank and was partly destroyed and partly put to flight. At about 12.30 p.m. the commander of the tank observed the retirement of Allied infantry in front of Cachy. He immediately turned northwards, halted the infantry, and then advanced on Cachy. About 800 metres from the village, seven enemy tanks suddenly appeared. Two of these were set on fire by Leutnant Bitter and a third was put out of action. The remaining four were bombarded by him and fled. In the meantime the gun, as a result of the breaking of two springs, was out of action. The retreating enemy tanks were pursued with machine-gun fire to within 200 metres of Cachy. Fire was then brought to bear on the north-eastern outskirts of the village. The infantry had meanwhile advanced once more on Cachy, but the village was not assaulted. At 3.45 p.m. the tank returned to its rendezvous, having fought continuously since 7 a.m.

Losses: one officer killed; five NCOs and men killed; one man missing; 13 NCOs and men wounded.

Compiled from German sources by Maj.-Gen. J.F.C. Fuller

CHAPTER SIX

Hamel

Once the German offensive had spent itself, the Allies, now driven back almost as far as Amiens, recovered their strength and prepared for a major counterattack. However, before this was possible it proved necessary to mount a series of operations to tidy up the line. Tanks figured in most of these actions but none was more notable than Hamel, a village just south of the Somme, which was attacked on 4 July. The tanks, working with Australian and American infantry in a copybook predawn action, were of the new Mark V type, and they were able to exploit their improved manoeuvrability to gain a memorable success.

The French, meanwhile, had developed tanks of their own. The original models were slow and cumbersome, but in 1917 a small, two-man machine was designed in conjunction with Renault which proved far more effective. Designed to be used en masse, the little tanks were much better suited to the more open style of fighting that characterized the last months of the war. A typical action follows. The Renaults were powered by a four-cylinder engine and only weighed 6.5 tons. They lacked the trench-crossing capability of heavier machines but made up for this with greater speed and mobility, plus the considerable advantage of a rotating turret which could mount a small 37 mm cannon or heavy machine gun.

The British Mark V, although outwardly similar to earlier models, was far superior in its mechanical design. Powered by a new and more powerful Ricardo engine, it also featured a form of transmission designed by Walter Wilson which enabled one man, from the crew of eight, to handle all the driving controls unaided. Now there was no need to halt in order to change direction and longer distances could be covered with far less strain upon the crew.

304 COMPANY, 2ME BATTALION DES CHARS LÉGERS, 501ME RÉGIMENTS D'ARTILLERIE SPÉCIALE, 31 MAY 1918

We embussed at Champlieu Camp as night fell on 30 May. It was not until daybreak next day that the first tanks of 304 Company arrived at St Pierre Aigle.

Renault FT17 light tanks transported in Exshaw steam lorries of the French Army moving up to the battle front.

We were carried in trucks drawn by vehicles of every sort. The drivers were very weary as they had only just returned from another convoy. The tanks were got off without incident and at once camouflaged.

About 9 o'clock the battalion commander arrived at the company. With his map open he gave his orders to the company commander in the presence of the section commanders:

> The attack will take place at midday. You will engage the enemy wherever met. Latest reports indicate that he is along the great Soissons–Paris road. The tall trees bordering it you can see over there. Your company will be on the left of the battalion. The battalion mission is to dislodge the enemy from the plateau of Ploisy and the ravines of Chazelle.

The company commander went forward to seek vainly to get in touch with the infantry. The section commanders went in the enemy direction to look for a possible route. But time was short. At 9.30 a.m. we had to be back to prepare for the advance. Owing to delays and incidents during transport, the company could put two sections only into line.

At 10 o'clock, in bright sunlight, in full view of an enemy observation balloon, we started the approach march across a slope covered with fields of corn. The ears of corn reached up to the turrets and thus masked the glitter of the moving tracks, which could not otherwise have escaped air observation.

The first bound was to end at Dommiers. We were to halt along the length of the cemetery hidden under apple trees. It was now nearly 11 a.m. and we were only about two miles from our front line.

The two section commanders were with the company commander reconnoitring. The country was the same as on the first bound, but the horizon was masked in front by a curtain of trees bordering the road. On our right lay the farm of Cravancon.

The company commander then announced, 'I shall go into action in my tank between the two sections.' The section we were to follow, that is the right section, had as its direction and final objective the northern part of the ravines of Chazelle. It was to leave for a neighbouring section a gap of 300 yards between its right and the farm. The section commander briefly gave the above directions to his crew commanders, who were at his side.

'Mount.'

The section commander remained dismounted with two signallers.

'Prepare to advance.'

The section in column was lined up to face the objective, then deployed into battle formation. It halted under cover 150 yards from the route to await zero.

It was now zero minus twenty.

This approach march was made without incident, except for a few odd shells which seemed to be merely ricochets. Very different from the approach marches we had known in 1917 during attacks on organized positions. There, bursts of enemy shells made an inferno of our approach, only ceasing when we reached the enemy lines, taken up with added intensity on our return. It was now 11.45. The signallers gave the warning order for departure. The section commander mounted and gave the signal. Advance. The ground on the enemy side seemed to be the same as that of the approach march, high fields of corn mingled with open plough. That is all we could see at the time.

The route contained certain steep banks, crossable after reconnaissance. The section commander got out of his tank and guided it across. From time to time the section commander and infantry battalion commander met. Contact was established much in these terms.

'We are off again. You follow us. Away we go then.'

At midday we moved out of the corn, crossed some open fields and then into

A group of Renaults with their crews preparing for action. All are equipped with 37 mm cannon, but whereas the centre tank has a cast turret the other two are of the built-up type.

the corn again. The section was now in no-man's land. No enemy were to be seen. We did not hear the noise of the shells bursting in front of us, but the number of craters still smoking, which turned aside the march of the tanks, gave evidence of the density of our barrage. Without stopping their tanks crew commanders fired a few shells or machine-gun bursts without any precise targets. The combination of fire and movement gave them confidence in themselves. Very soon we saw passing to the rear of us little groups of the enemy, haggard, hands above their heads, without equipment. The effect of our attack had been complete.

The section was halted by signal. We must have a look around. By opening the turret visor we were able to see that all the cars had arrived. We were firing but little. Behind us in the wake of the tanks visible amongst the corn little groups of riflemen were advancing. Towards the end of this run we saw around us the corn stalks shaking and men crawling about on all fours undecided what to do. But we did not fire. We had just crossed a line of advanced posts. In their retreat the enemy detachments had cleared the field of fire of a more solid line we would shortly be up against.

The signal was given, 'Advance.' After a few hundred yards suddenly the corn

A section of machine gun-armed Renaults moving into action.

ceased. We were in open, uncultivated ground. As soon as we debouched we were subjected to heavy machine-gun fire directed particularly against the slits and port holes. The hammer of bullets against the armour, accompanied by splash, showed us the general direction of the fire. In our case fire was coming from the left. Many bullets struck the gun shield and made traversing difficult. But we swung the turret and there was the machine gun, not more than 50 yards away. It took five rounds to put it out, and the tracks completed the work. All the tanks were now on the same alignment. They were all in action firing and manoeuvring, which showed us that we were on the enemy's line of resistance.

Where have the infantry got to? They have not passed the last cornfield. Yet we are not now under fire. We must go back and see what is happening. Perhaps the infantry is still under fire. This seems to be so since, as we withdraw, the hammering of bullets on our side resumes, but very much less dense. It was by no means easy to approach the tanks. The inclination was to keep away. Bullets ricocheting off the armour created a most unpleasant zone all round us. Eventually the section commander wrote a message which he put in a shell case and threw out of the turret door. It was picked up but remained without apparent reply. The message was brief, it read: 'Where are the machine-guns which are holding you up? Follow us we are going back to take them on.'

The section did not, of course, return as a whole. That was not the section commander's idea. The other tanks remained in position, giving the impression that they were waiting for a signal from their leader. Those that could find cover were firing. The others were anxious not to offer a sitting target. They were describing figures of eight and carrying out the fire and movement drill.

Again the signal, 'Advance.'

This time we advanced amongst arms and trophies flung down by the enemy in his retreat. We fired a few rounds against the features from which automatic fire appeared to come. Our infantry did not seem to be following up. They merely watched us draw away from them.

At the head of the ravine, at what appeared to be about 600 yards range, an anti-tank gun unmasked. We saw the flash of discharge. It was evidently firing at us. The first rounds fell in quick succession in front of us. They appeared to be duds. They rolled over and over in clouds of dust but did not burst. Without halting the crew commander opened fire against the gun, which replied vigorously. In the course of this duel a shell pitched just in front of the tank, powdering with a hot and dusty smoke the faces of the crew at the portholes. But the mobile gun was a match for the stationary. With a quick tack the tank dodged behind some bushes and from this cover a few well directed rounds quickly silenced the enemy's fire. We advanced again, zig-zagging towards the cannon, which did not reply.

The section commander therefore accelerated to rejoin the section. Having seen no signal they had gone on. The anti-tank gun had picked on the section commander's tank. We found out afterwards that a shell had gone right through the tail. We found out also that only two tanks had seen the gun. The section commander had not waited to order a concentration of fire but had himself at once engaged. This action allowed his subordinates to get on. Little groups of our own riflemen now appeared, mostly Colonial troops. Rifles in hand they regarded us with curiosity. It would appear that they might have engaged the anti-tank gun. They must have seen the flash and heard the discharge. Now we arrived in sight of the ravine, the final objective. There it was in full view, not forgetting the anti-tank gun. It was on wheels, probably a 77 mm, partly dismantled by the tank. Many of the crew lay dead beside it. In the middle distance in the ravine we saw another piece, or perhaps a limber. It served us as a target.

All together the tanks of the battalion breasted the crest of the ravine. A few shells were fired at fugitives with apparent effect. For some time, in complete absence of fire, the tanks in defensive position under cover of scrub and

Renaults and infantry advancing.

undergrowth, awaited the arrival of the infantry. It was nearly 3 o'clock when groups of riflemen rejoined us. Contact was established by a few words shouted from the turret.

Flag signal, 'Rally.' All tanks of the battalion scuttled to the rear. Back we went by the same track, dismounting when we reached the road, the crews full of confidence and happy in having accomplished their mission. In line ahead, crew commanders dismounted, we returned to St Pierre Aigle. There maintenance was at once undertaken. We must be ready for all eventualities.

Capitaine Aubert, Section Commander, 304 Company

13TH BATTALION, 4 JULY 1918

South of the Somme the line held by the Australian Corps in front of Villers-Bretonneux was to some extent dominated by a spur running from the main plateau to the river. Vaire Wood and Hamel Wood made additional strongpoints in the enemy positions in front of this spur, and the ruins of Hamel village still afforded cover. It was therefore decided to carry the high ground east of Hamel, which would give very important observation, not only up the Somme but also to the south-east and north-east, and would afford a useful jumping-off place for any subsequent advance. The operation was of minor importance and of limited objective, but offered two special points of interest; it was the first definitely offensive operation undertaken on the British front since the German advance began, and it was, further, the first appearance in the attack of the improved type of tank, the Mark V. The high command consented to the employment of tanks on a scale that was large in proportion to the front attacked, the saving of casualties to the infantry being made the most important factor in the plan. The operation was entrusted to the Australian 4th Division, with whom four companies of American infantry were to make their first entry in the war. The tank attack was at first intended to be carried out by the 8th Tank Battalion under Lt-Col. the Hon. J.D.Y. Bingham, but by degrees the scheme was enlarged and first one, and finally two, companies of the 13th Battalion were added to the force employed.

C Company (Maj. Foster) had carried out four days of training at the practice ground at Vaux en Amenois and on 28 June took part in a tactical scheme in

An oblique view of the approaches to Hamel taken three weeks after the battle. Notice how artillery has concentrated on the crossroads.

combination with Australian infantry. On the two following days all officers of the company made a reconnaissance of the ground on the Hamel front, and on the evening of 30 June the tanks of the company made their first approach march from Allonville Wood into the forward area. B Company (Maj. Griffin) received much less notice and had only three days available for reconnaissance, two approach marches, and the move to the starting point. In both companies all movement was made by night. Surprise being the first essential for the success of the operation, every possible precaution was taken to conceal from the enemy all signs of the presence of tanks in the forward area. Abnormal movement of any kind during the day was rigorously suppressed.

By the night of 2 July both companies were in their final positions, B Company at Fouilloy and C Company disposed, for reasons which will appear later, in two half companies, of which one lay near Hamelet on the Somme, the other some further 1,200 yards south-west.

The plan of attack was kept as simple as possible in view of the employment of tanks. Two and a half brigades of infantry were detailed for the task, and five companies of tanks, sixty in all, were available to assist them. The total frontage of the advance was approximately 6,000 yards, increasing to 7,500 yards on the furthest objective, and the greatest depth to be penetrated was about 2,500 yards. It will be noted that the number of infantry employed, one battalion to each thousand yards, was very small, but, as the result showed, ample for the purpose. Zero hour was fixed for 3.10 a.m. on 4 July. At this hour it was considered there would be just sufficient light to distinguish friend from foe at short distances, while the advance of the tanks over the crest of the hill would be concealed from the enemy's view.

The operation was to be conducted as a direct advance of tanks and infantry under cover of a field gun barrage, with the heavy artillery barrage in depth moving ahead. Vaire Wood and Hamel were to be passed on either flank by the troops for the final objective, one battalion with its own tanks being detailed to mop up each of these points. It was arranged that the barrage preceding the tanks should consist of 60 per cent shrapnel, 30 per cent high explosive and 10 per cent smoke shell. Tanks were to start from positions about 1,000 yards behind the infantry, who were themselves 200 yards behind the start line of the barrage. Tanks had thus 1,200 yards to cover to reach the barrage start line. This was timed to lift four minutes after zero, moving forward 100 yards every three minutes to the first halt line, thence 100 yards every four minutes to the final objective. The noise of the tanks' approach was to be concealed in two ways: aeroplanes were detailed to fly up and down the whole army front while tanks were moving to their starting points, and for the twenty minutes before zero, when tanks would be advancing towards the infantry line. Harassing fire by

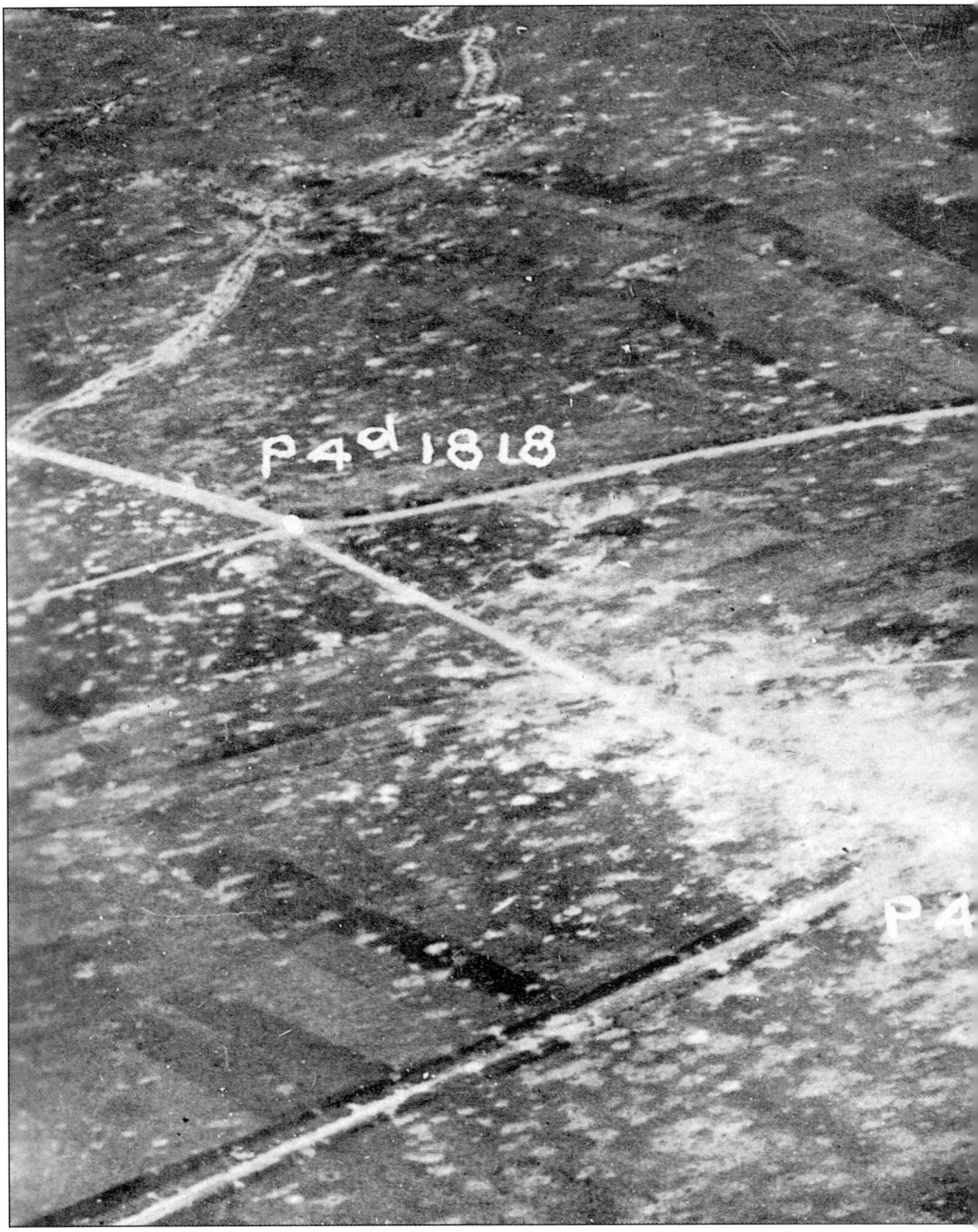
P4d 1818
P4

HAMEL

artillery and machine guns during the early hours of the morning was also ordered with the same object. The enemy was carefully drilled in this action of planes and guns for some days prior to the attack. The use of tanks made all preliminary bombardment unnecessary.

The sixty tanks were disposed in two waves. The attack on the main objective was to be carried out by the 8th Battalion, while B Company of the 13th followed in support. To prevent the flanks of the advance being pinched in, one half company of the 13th with a battalion of infantry was ordered to operate outwards towards each flank of the objective. Maj. Foster's company was assigned this duty, and the distance between the two spheres of action being considerable, the direction of the half company on the right flank was handed over at short notice to Capt H.E. Morritt, Maj. Foster's second-in-command. The function of Maj. Griffin's company was twofold. Following 300 yards behind the first wave, it was available either to mop up opposition which might spring to life after the first wave had passed, or to fill gaps and replace casualties in the front line itself. At the barrage halt line, 900 yards from the start, the tanks were to be merged in the front line for the final assault, taking the places of tanks engaged in mopping up Hamel and Vaire Wood.

At 10.30 p.m. on 3 July tanks began to move up to their start lines and were all in position by 1 a.m. on the 4th. B Company had approximately 2,000 yards to cover and completed the march in one and a half hours. The enemy betrayed no signs of uneasiness and the taping of routes to the infantry start line was carried out without interruption. Eight minutes before zero tanks started for the attack, picked up their infantry and pressed forward. The barrage fell at zero, the heavy guns at the same time engaging known artillery positions along the whole army front, with special attention directed to the strong enemy concentrations in the Cerisy valley.

The attack was a complete success; the enemy was taken entirely by surprise and the cooperation of all arms worked out exactly as planned. The morning was very dark at zero hour and the lack of light, combined with the dense smoke and thick dust raised by the barrage, at first made it difficult for the tanks to pick their way, to keep direction and especially to develop their fire successfully. The enemy infantry offered small opposition and freely surrendered to the tanks and the Australians with them. Enemy machine-gunners, on the other hand, as usual made a stout resistance. The greater handiness of the Mark V tank was of the utmost value in dealing with these, many cases being recorded of tanks running over and crushing the guns, which were frequently kept in action by their crews until the tank was actually on top of the gun position. Over two hundred machine guns were accounted for in this area. The presence of standing crops made their concealment easy and had prevented their detection by air photographs.

A Mark V male tank, photographed the day after the battle, moving through a village near Hamel which was taken by American and Australian troops.

The tanks of B Company, driving forward at zero at their best speed, caught up the leading tanks of the 8th Battalion at the halt line and pressed on ahead of the infantry to the final objective. Many fine examples of individual courage and resource were shown, of which it is only possible to quote a few examples. 2/Lt G.A. Edward came upon an enemy dug-out which he could not reach with his tank and from which the occupants were firing at him. With one man, Pte J. Benns, he left the tank and attacked the enemy on foot. Between them they killed seven of the garrison with their revolvers and compelled the remainder to surrender. Two officers of this company, 2/Lts Mayo and Rawlinson, were brought to notice for fixing towing ropes to disabled tanks under fire and successfully getting them out of action. 2/Lt Porter, having reached his final objective and wanting information as to the further needs of the infantry, got out of his tank under fire and consulted with the nearest infantry commander. Being told that enemy snipers were giving trouble from standing crops in the foreground he went forward with his tank and searched the crops with case shot; a number of the enemy bolted and were dealt with by the light Hotchkiss guns. Of twelve tanks of this company, ten reached their final objectives, one being hit by a shell while on the move and the other ditched in a quarry north-west of Hamel village. These were successfully brought back to the rallying point after the action. The position having been taken, the tanks patrolled behind a protective barrage until released by the infantry commanders on the spot. Most of them had prisoners, captured guns and other trophies to show as a result of the action. The company rallied after the fight in a gully of the Somme valley between Fouilly and Blangy. Nearly all the tanks had been struck by armour-piercing bullets and showed other signs of hard fighting, but with one exception were in condition to fight again; the crews, after forty eight hours of continuous work, were thoroughly exhausted.

The half company of C on the left was operating with battalions of the 6th Australian Brigade. All tanks of these two sections reached the starting point, though one delayed by mechanical trouble was only brought forward at the last moment by the energy of 2/Lt Kay, the company engineer. Their objectives being on the river flank, the outer tanks encountered little opposition and patrolled the infantry front without seeing much of the enemy. The inner section had more to do, as their objectives included a quarry organized as a strongpoint. 2/Lt Dower, after overcoming a number of machine-gun nests, was ditched at this point, in front of his objective. Setting his crew to dig the tank out, he started to collect prisoners to carry on this work and returned in a few minutes with some fifty of these, some of whom were employed in digging until the tank was free. All tanks of this half company rallied with no casualties.

On the right, or pivot, flank, Capt Morritt's section had some heavy fighting and met with severe shell fire from the south-east after the objectives had been won. Lt Berry, finding that his infantry were embarrassed by a post in front of the objective, led his tank on foot to attack it. He shot with his revolver the crew of a machine gun which he captured and carried back himself to his tank. 2/Lt Geraghty was wounded and his tank put out of action by a shell; this tank was subsequently towed out by 2/Lt Gill. 2/Lt Hulton's tank broke down with mechanical trouble under full observation of the enemy. Captains Morritt and Larkins both made their way under fire to the tank and found that a new part was required before it could move. A spare part was obtained by 2/Lt Kay, who went forward with Capt Larkins, still through shell fire, to the tank, installed the new part and brought the tank home.

By 6 p.m. all tanks of 13th Battalion were at their rallying points. Four officers and eight other ranks had been wounded, of whom two officers and three other ranks remained at duty.

The Australian infantry were delighted with the tanks. Their casualties had been light and of these the bulk were incurred among those battalions which had preferred to move ahead of the tanks into action. In addition, tanks had

A Mark V halted by the roadside as a field gun edges past.

saved the infantry a vast amount of labour. Each fighting tank brought up two boxes of ammunition, and filled Lewis-gun drums and tins of drinking water. A further four carrier tanks delivered near the objective, within half an hour of its capture, a total weight of 50,000 lb of wire, pickets, sheet iron, bombs, ammunition and water equal, at 40 lb per man, to a saving of 1,250 men employed as carriers, a factor which particularly appealed to the Australians.

The outstanding feature of the action was economy – for the infantry economy in lives and labour, and for the guns economy in shells and effort – and this saving was due to the tanks. But the success was due to the combination of all arms. The Australian staff work was a model of skill and attention to detail; the cooperation of infantry, guns, airmen and tanks was excellent; the secret was successfully guarded; the barrage was overwhelming; and the determination and dash of tank crews and the astonishing infantry did the rest. The list of captures included two 77 mm guns, twenty-six trench mortars, over two hundred machine guns, and two anti-tank rifles of a new type, with which the 13th Battalion was destined later to be more acquainted. Of the enemy personnel, 41 officers and 1,431 other ranks were taken.

Mark V male tank H52, which lost a track during the battle, photographed near Hamel, 4 July 1918.

On the evening of the battle, about 10.30 p.m., an enemy aeroplane dropped three bombs into the gully in which both companies had rallied, inflicting losses on those sections which had fought on the right flank. The two section commanders, Captains Walker and Larkins, were killed, as were Lt Berry and 2/Lt Atack and three other ranks. 2/Lt Hulton and three other ranks were wounded, and the officer and two of the men died on the following day. It is probable that the real objective of the attacking plane was certain gun emplacements hard by, but it must be admitted that these officers, worn out by their exceptional exertions, had taken insufficient care to protect themselves on their return. The lesson was not lost on the battalion.

On 5 July both companies were withdrawn across the Somme by Daours Ridge and returned to Querrieu Wood. Two accidents to tank commanders on the line of march brought to notice a new danger due to the speed of the Mark V tank. 2/Lt Harris, jumping from his tank to the ground, slipped and fell; the track ran over his right leg which was badly fractured. On the same march 2/Lt Porter was guiding his tank down the dip into a sunken road when the tank fell foward on to him, inflicting injuries of which he subsequently died. An order issued as a result of these accidents laid down that guides must always be accompanied by a second man and must keep a distance of 20 yards ahead; jumping from the tank while on the move was forbidden. The triumph of successful action had ended on a sad note.

9TH BATTALION, 23 JULY 1918

The 9th Battalion had been, from April – when it had been rearmed with Mark V tanks which replaced the old Mark IVs of Cambrai fame – to July, in the Hebuterne sector, the three companies being scattered over a wide front waiting for Ludendorff's next shock, which never came. Without any warning, on the night of 18–19 July, the tanks trekked for an unknown destination, all other personnel and stores being bundled into 3 ton lorries and headed for somewhere into the night. Next day we loaded tanks and personnel at a railhead near Beauquesne, and after a journey of a few hours left the train and parked up close by in a wood. On the night 20th–21st a rather long trek brought the tanks to the last stop before the lying-up point, a wood which was reached about midnight.

With their sponsons withdrawn to conform with the loading gauge, a train-load of Mark Vs waits to leave a railhead.

Mark V tanks trekking from a railhead. The new engine and transmission made these tanks much less tiring to drive over long distances than the old Mark IVs.

At this stop we were visited by our Brigade Commander, Brigadier General Courage, who told us we were to do a stunt with a picked division of French troops, the modern representatives of Napoleon's Grenadiers, who could be relied upon to keep up with the tanks in the attack. In conclusion General Courage adjured us to 'blood our tracks'.

On the night of 21st–22nd the tanks, travelling the hard roads and country between in fourth gear, made walking beside them impossible, so everybody perched on the unditching beams and had a nice ride to the lying-up point, which was in a wood about 1,000 yards or so from the show ground. No fires being allowed, cooked food was brought up from the last halting place in large Thermos containers; all personnel rested during the day and orders were issued that no one was to quit the wood or go near its fringe in case of observation from the German kite balloons which were flying fairly close.

The day was fine and, as befitting the coming storm, calm also, in spite of the fact that the tanks had punched their way up to this position in top gear. Of course French aircraft did their stuff, droning over the area the whole time. The battalion was equipped with 36 tanks, and there were half a dozen or so from the Driving School at Sautrecourt in waiting.

On the night of 22nd–23rd the battalion was joined by the French personnel, all volunteers who could speak English, one to each tank. These men were to communicate between the crews and the 3rd French Division, who comprised the infantry in the attack. The position of these volunteers was on the fan casing at the back of the tank; also, I believe for the first time, the three distinguishing flags were used by each tank. The Frenchmen were very emphatic about their intention of waving the tricoloured one in token of victory. On 23 July, the anniversary of the battalion's arrival in France, the tanks went into battle in three phases at slightly different times, the idea being for one company to take over and push on when the preceding one had reached its objective. In this way poor old C Company took over from A just as Mr Hun recovered from his surprise, which was complete as usual. Attaining their objective the tanks began to patrol in front of their infantry to enable them to consolidate the newly gained ground as much as possible. All this time the usual blizzard, or shell curtain, was coming down around the devoted tanks, whose French personnel did their bit loyally and in some cases incautiously, with the back flaps of the tanks open, waving the *Tricolore* and exhorting their infantry. Several of these crew Frenchmen were killed or wounded; one who had lived in Canada, and spoke like a Canadian, was found by his crew hanging half out of the tank with his head blown off.

Mark V tanks, actually of 10th Battalion, advancing with infantry over unspoiled country.

To return to C Company, one tank had not got away from the jumping off point, and of the eleven others six were knocked out, chiefly by direct hits over open sights. Most of the casualties occured after evacuating the knocked out tanks. The most amazing thing of all was that although tanks must have been seen by the enemy emerging from and returning to the lying up point at various intervals from daybreak to dusk and, moreover, the remainder of the battalion, with tanks, did not quit the locality till after dark, about 10 p.m., not one round of shell fire was dropped on the hornet's nest throughout our stay of 45 hours, nor was there any bombing.

The immediate military object of the operation was to establish a bridgehead, the accomplishment of which, it was understood, was effected to the satisfaction of our stage management; yet, although to the ordinary soldier this may have appeared to be the ostensible reason, one has cause to believe that the real reason was to influence the French more favourably as regards tanks and their value in warfare. I believe this particular object was attained.

The conduct of the crews, in their role as the spearhead of the battle, maintained the high standard of our infant corps. The presentation of the badge of the 3rd French Division, to be worn by all ranks of the battalion, and the thanks of the French Corps Commander, followed at a parade when the success of the venture was announced as resulting in the capture of four guns, 300 machine guns and 1,500 prisoners. Also a measure of *vin rouge* was issued by the French to all ranks by way of celebration.

RQMS H.G. Mackenzie, 9th Battalion

CHAPTER SEVEN

Amiens

The Battle of Amiens, which commenced in the early-morning mist of 8 August 1918, was the final blow from which the German Army never recovered. Staged without any preliminary bombardment, 450 tanks were launched against the German lines with the effect of total surprise, and proved to the German High Command that the war would have to be concluded, in the Allies' favour.

Two other armoured vehicles, acting in support of the heavy tanks, made distinct impressions during the battle. Whippet tanks assisted the cavalry and in one case caused havoc well behind the German lines, while armoured cars made even deeper raids into enemy territory with outstanding results. A third type, the Gun-Carrier tank, now mostly relegated to supply-carrying duties, suffered disastrously on the eve of the battle but this did not affect the final outcome.

The Gun-Carrier appeared in prototype form in March 1917 and some were available at the time of Cambrai. They could transport a sixty-pounder gun or transport and fire a 6 in. howitzer but opportunities to do this being few, they proved much more successful in a supply-carrying role. The design, dominated by the need to stow a large gun, set them apart from any other type of tank, but in mechanical terms they were similar to the Mark IV, with a Daimler engine and four-man driving team.

1ST GUN-CARRIER COMPANY, TANK CORPS, 6 AUGUST 1918

On the night of 6 August 17 tanks moved up to the orchard which lies on the northern outskirts of the town of Villers-Bretonneux and three tanks to Hamelet. The tanks were on this occasion to operate with the infantry and were all loaded with infantry supplies, including large numbers of primed bombs.

The tanks in the orchard at Villers-Bretonneux were left in charge of a guard while personnel retired to the north-east corner of the Bois de l'Abbaye to rest in preparation for the following day's activities. During the afternoon of the 7th, while the officers and men were lazily watching and commenting upon the shell fire which the Boche was distributing in a desultory manner over the town and surrounding countryside, a column of flame and smoke was seen to shoot skywards from the heart of the orchard. At first there was some doubt whether the tanks had been hit or whether the Boche had fired a dump of ammunition but all uncertainty quickly vanished when a second burst of flame and smoke rose above the distant trees, the dull roar of the explosion rang across the intervening stretch of sun-baked country and fragments of a tank were seen hurtling through the air. Cheered by their spectacular success the enemy gunners now concentrated upon the orchard and before the runner, despatched by the NCO in charge of the guard, could reach the Sections, or those who had volunteered to help could reach the scene of destruction, several more tanks either exploded or burst into flames.

Within a very short space of time a party of officers and men were on the scene to give what help was possible in saving the tanks still remaining. But the sight presented to their gaze was sufficient to daunt even the most courageous. Several tanks were burning fiercely, their petrol tanks having been pierced and the contents set alight. In all directions loads of bombs were exploding with loud reports. At any moment the gun cotton charges carried on each tank for demolition purposes might catch, and from overhead fell a torrent of shrapnel and high explosive. One more tank exploded and the party dropped in the ditch behind the orchard hedge while tons of metal were hurled high in the air and the cargo of bursting bombs whistled past their heads. The heat from exploding and burning tanks burnt black the hedge before them, but there still remained several tanks untouched and into the heart of this lurid inferno dashed the rescue party.

Two of the wrecked Gun-Carrier supply tanks in the devastated orchard at Villers-Bretonneux.

What followed may be imagined better than described. Those who took part found themselves vaguely wondering after the event what had really transpired. Their actions were the desperate resource of frenzied necessity – born on the spur of the moment and lived in an unnatural dream – a nightmare of hell from which memory subsequently recoiled. From confused narratives a few facts stand out clearly. The corporal in charge of the guard, being on the scene, was one of the first to make an effort. He and one other started up an engine. The corporal mounted the driver's seat but it was necessary to swing the tank in order to move her away from the holocaust and in spite of every effort the gears refused to respond. A warning came that the tank had been hit and the pair jumped clear at the moment she burst into flames. A shell bursting overhead wounded the corporal in the neck and he was removed to the dressing station with the unpleasant reflection that his gallant effort had been in vain. In attempting to drive another tank the force of the explosion lifted a sergeant out of the driver's cab and deposited him, badly bruised and shocked but otherwise unhurt, several yards from the tank. The smoke formed so thick a fog in the orchard that another party commenced operations on a tank before they could

Not all the Gun-Carriers were destroyed at Villers-Bretonneux. *Harwich*, serving in the supply role, was photographed in Bucquoy later in the month.

see that it was already on fire. The workers however refused to be daunted and did not cease operations until three tanks were safely out of the way and the remaining ones beyond hope of recovery.

Everybody had displayed courage and gallantry in their actions to a high degree and 2/Lt G.H. Smith was awarded the Military Cross and Sgt Strang a bar to the Distinguished Conduct Medal which he had previously won for good all-round work with his section in the Ypres Salient. Fourteen tanks were completely destroyed on this memorable afternoon and the hope which had run high among the officers and men that the company would make history during the coming operations faded away. The remaining tanks, however, were to adhere to the original arrangements and their crews were the envy of those whose tanks were now a thing of the past.

6TH BATTALION

On the evening of 6 August the battalion started for its first battle as a Whippet battalion, on a trek to Amiens with forty-eight Whippets and fully trained personnel. The mere thought of a trek to Amiens from Bois de Naours with

A Whippet going forward, with two of its crew taking the air. Extra petrol cans are strapped on the front.

Mark IVs would have dismayed everyone, but with Whippets it was comparatively easy. Amiens was reached late at night and the tanks were parked up in one of the boulevards leading out towards Villers-Bretonneux, while billets were found for all ranks in a school close by.

At midnight on 7 August the battalion left Amiens for the forward positions and reached our front line at 6.30 a.m. on the morning of 8 August. The line of advance was along the railway running from Villers-Bretonneux to Chaulnes. B Company would operate on the north and C Company on the south, while A Company would be in reserve. Each company had approximately 2,500 yards frontage. Of the forty-eight tanks starting from Amiens for the final stages of the approach march, forty-four arrived at Trones Wood. B Company were in position at La Bastille Mill by 8 a.m.; C Company reached Marcelcave, their starting point, about the same time. Lt Col. Truman gave B and C Companies their final orders and returned to where A Company were in reserve. When it was certain that the battle was progressing satisfactorily Col. Truman gave A Company orders to move in the direction of Caix.

About 9.15 a.m. a Whippet, going over a dud shell, caused it to explode, wounding Col. Truman and Maj. Inglis. Maj. Wood then took over command of the battalion.

On approaching the western side of Guillaucourt the infantry were hung up by heavy machine-gun fire. There is a valley running north from the river Luce, ending in the village of Guillaucourt. It was here, and from the high ground to the east, that the opposition was coming. Maj. West ordered six Whippets to wheel left up this valley and attack Guillaucourt from the south, while three others worked round and attacked from the north. Some batteries of artillery were captured in this valley. At 11.30 a.m. Maj. West sent the following signal from a point east of Guillaucourt:

> Nine C Company Whippets were on the Red Line at 10.15. Snipers and machine guns on the low ground south of Guillaucourt. No cavalry have yet appeared. 1st Cavalry Brigade north of the railway have gone on. Cannot get in touch as too much machine-gun fire and sniping north of line. We are progressing rapidly. 11.30 a.m.

Shortly after he met the GOC, 9th Cavalry Brigade at a point 1,000 yards south of Marcelcave and was able to organize an attack on the railway running north-east–south-west. The enemy clung to the woods but was eventually chased out.

Meanwhile, Maj. Rycroft, commanding B Company, detached four tanks to cooperate with the cavalry in clearing Bayonvilliers. The action was most satisfactorily carried out. The company had now deployed north of the railway, extending over some 2,500 yards. They went forward with the cavalry, obtaining very good practice on all kinds of targets. Just south of Harbonnières the Queen's Bays made a charge on some gun teams and transport. Several of B Company's tanks took part. Farther on, to the east of Harbonnières, a considerable amount of transport was caught on the road. By means of the combined operations of the cavalry and tanks, about five hundred prisoners were captured as they tried to escape eastwards. The pursuit was followed up by two tanks under Lt C.B. Arnold and Lt A.L. Watkins. Lt Arnold's tank, A344, failed to return and was discovered next day lying burnt out. It was ascertained afterwards that the 60th Australian Infantry Brigade had been held up on the railway south of Harbonnières and had applied to Lt Arnold for assistance. After having got the infantry forward his tank received a direct hit. His driver, Pte Carney, was killed but Lt Arnold and the other member of his crew were wounded and captured after putting up so stiff a fight that forty dead Germans were afterwards found around the tank.

Both B and C Companies, in their progress, were able to account for several batteries of guns. To assist in the final dispersion of the enemy the officer commanding C Company despatched three tanks to patrol as far as Rosières.

Troops stop in their work to watch a Whippet as it goes into action.

Another tank was despatched to the bridge on the railway near Harbonnières where the enemy had made a desperate attempt to hold on and hang up our advance. The two tanks patrolling as far as Rosières came under extremely heavy machine-gun fire but were able to harass the enemy who were digging in on a defensive line to the west of this village. By reaching the line Vrely–Rosières–Warvillers, the tank patrols enabled the infantry to consolidate on the Amiens defence line.

A Company remained, as ordered, in reserve in the valley east of Marcelcave. The battalion was ordered to rally at Marcelcave. Forty tanks rallied at this point by 10 p.m. Two tanks of B Company were ditched near the railway south of Harbonnières; Nos 313 and 332. No. 344 was missing with Lt Arnold and crew. Tank 364, A Company, received a direct hit and was burnt out. No. 375, C Company, received a direct hit in the valley south of Guillaucourt and No. 357 was burnt out while following up the pursuit farther east of this village.

5TH TANK BRIGADE, 8 AUGUST 1918

The operation to be carried out by the Australian Corps was an attack on the front between the River Somme and the Villers-Bretonneux to Challons railway; the Canadian Corps were to operate on the right, and on the left III Corps, with whom was the 10th Tank Battalion, administered by the 5th Tank Brigade.

The attack was planned in two stages corresponding to the formation of the ground. A number of gullies run down from the high ground on the south to the river, of which two penetrate deeply across this front from Cerisy to Lamotte and from Morcourt almost to Harbonnières. The capture of the ground beyond these two features formed the two phases of the advance on this day, but a further outpost line, to which the infantry-carrying tanks could bring up machine-gunners, was designated in front of the final objective.

In the first phase of the attack a creeping barrage was to be employed, under cover of which tanks would bring forward their infantry to the first objective. The second phase was to start four hours after zero, and in this stage there was to be no barrage, but artillery would move up to engage known enemy positions. Air protection was provided to cover the noise of tanks while approaching and deploying. The greatest depth of advance was approximately 10,000 yards. In the first phase the attack was to be carried out by 2nd Australian Division on the right and 3rd Australian Division on the left. When this objective was reached, the 5th Australian Division was to pass through the 2nd for the next attack and the 4th Australian Division were similarly to pass through the 3rd. The 1st Australian Division remained in Corps reserve.

An oblique view, looking south-east towards Achiet le Grand over a hutted camp, taken about two weeks after the start of the battle. Three Whippet tanks and a Mark V can be seen close to the road in the foreground.

Approximately half of the Mark V tanks at the disposal of 5th Tank Brigade were allotted to each of the first two phases, but all survivors from the first stage were to rally and form a second wave in the further advance.

17TH BATTALION, 8 AUGUST 1918

The cars going to the south were more particularly entrusted with the task of clearing Framerville, which was known to be an enemy corps headquarters.

The raid was brilliantly successful. No. 8 Section, commanded by Lt Rollings, nailed the Australian flag on the German general's front door, though by that time there were but few enemy in the neighbourhood to admire it. Four mounted officers appeared during this proceeding and were accounted for by a single burst of fire.

The men of No. 6 Section, under Lt Herd, were meanwhile operating against columns of transport moving through the village in retreat and finding targets in

An Austin armoured car of 17th Battalion on a tree-lined road near Warfusee on 8 August 1918.

German soldiers coming casually out of the houses to see what the noise was about. Just past Framerville, where the road bends sharply, they ran into three artillery limbers. These were destroyed, men and horses alike. The same fate overtook the driver of a lorry. His car ran into a ditch and blocked the road.

The two sections then got into touch. As the road was, by this time, more of a shambles than a car route it was not possible to return by way of Vauvillers and Harbonnières. So they went back on their tracks to La Flaque, when they were joined by the cars which had gone north. The utter surprise effected by this raid may be judged by the fact that, during operations of six cars in and around Framerville, not a single shot was fired at them by the enemy.

The moral effect of war machines, moving at a great pace unscathed and apparently invulnerable, far behind the enemy lines and astride his communications, was incalculable. All soldiers know how rumours spread from the ration dump. It is not very difficult to trace the origin of the story of a new British tank that went into action at 30 miles an hour. The battalion was mentioned by a British communiqué, and a German one also – which shows we had got home. The Commanding Officer had the high honour of being personally congratulated by His Majesty the King a few days later on the achievements of the battalion in this action. His Majesty was motoring to

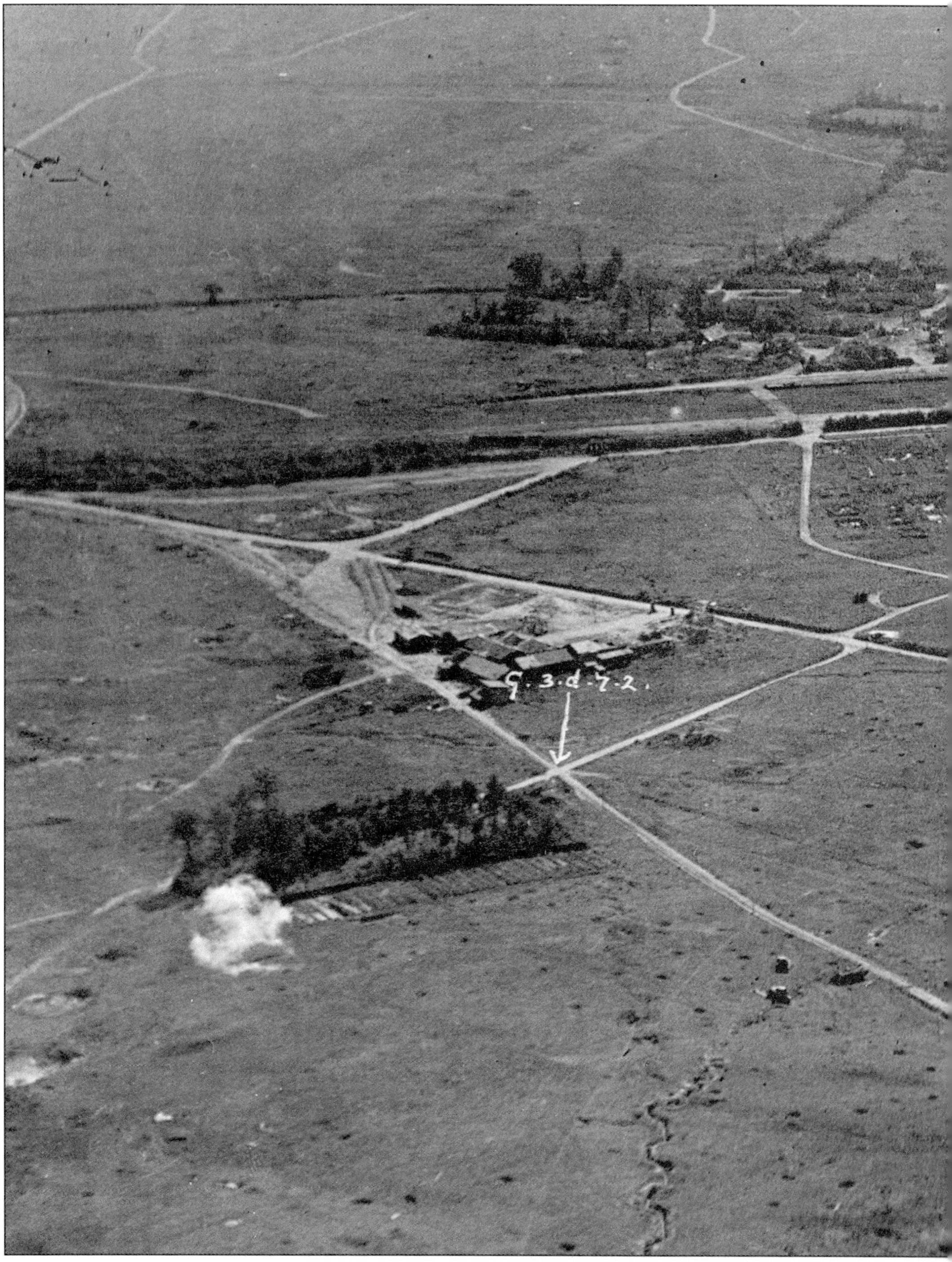
G.3.d.7.2.

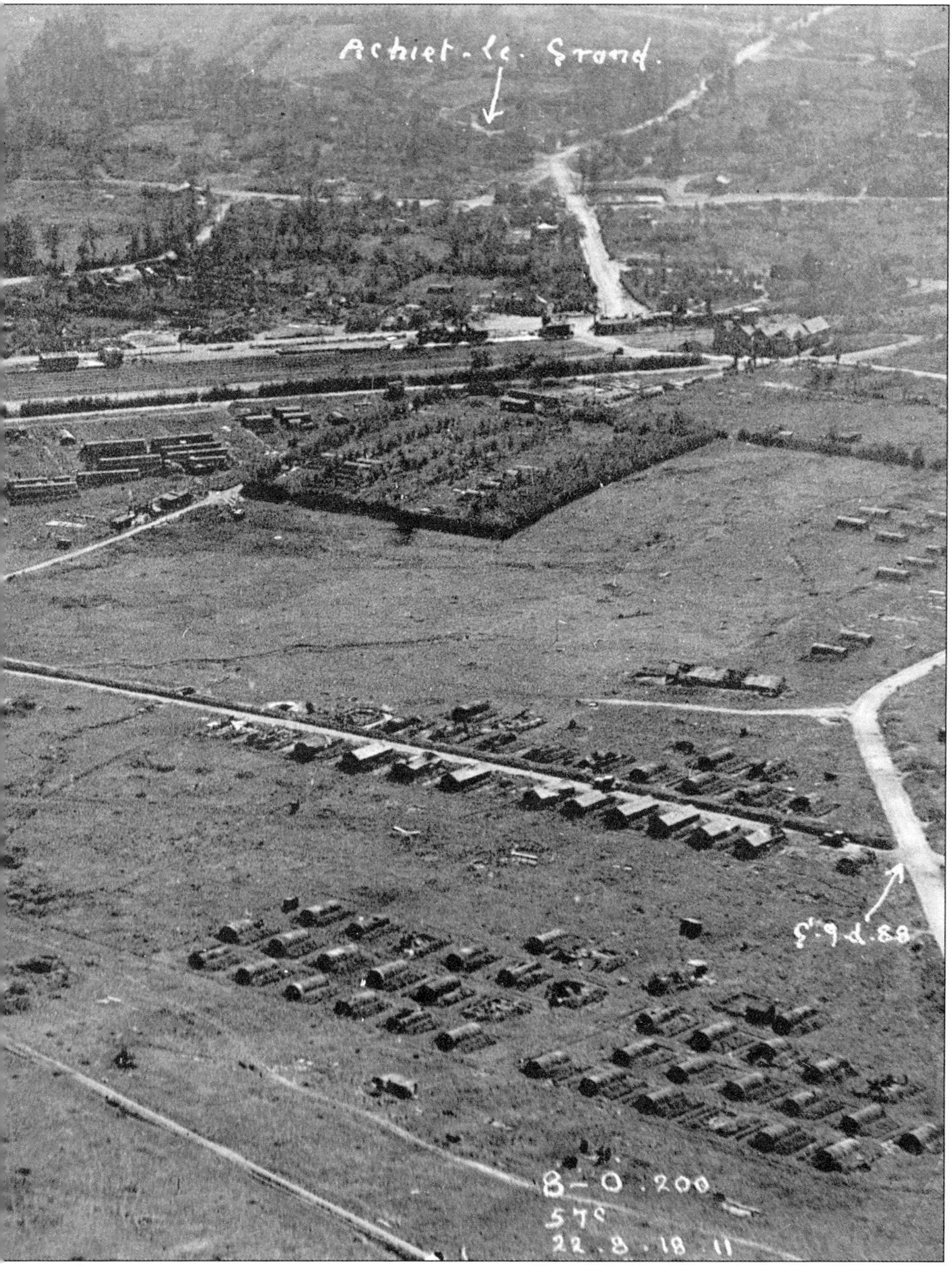
Achiet-le-Grand.
8-O.200
57c
22.8.18 11

Villers-Bretonneux and, seeing the armoured cars parked near the roadside, stopped his car and sent for an officer. Lt Herd was the officer on duty. His Majesty entered into a long conversation with him, asking him to give more details of incidents which he had already been informed of and also to relate particulars of what he had done with his own section in the great battle. Lt Herd was able to give him full details of the attack on Framerville, the recitation of which greatly amused and interested His Majesty.

TANK NO. 9003 *BARRHEAD*, 2ND BATTALION, 8 AUGUST 1918

Plans of the entire attack had been previously explained and every point discussed to ensure the complete success. Each tank was given a certain task to perform on the day of the attack. We were to operate with the 2nd Australian Division, our jumping-off point being slightly east of Villers-Bretonneux.

A typical tree-lined French highway in the battle area. This is the main road running east to St Quentin from Villers-Bretonneux, and the oblique view shows a stretch south of Proyart. The country around here was almost untouched by war.

On the evening of 7 August we left the tankodrome at 9 p.m. to take up our position on the jumping-off point ready for the attack next morning. The approach march is always a most important and trying part of the tanks' work. It must be done at night and every precaution has to be taken to prevent the enemy hearing our approach, as much of the success of the tanks' action depends on taking the enemy by surprise. The first part of the approach march was comparatively easy, but afterwards the route became more difficult, therefore guiding tapes were laid down under the supervision of officers detailed for the work. At a short distance from the jumping-off point we halted and were informed that the attack was to commence at 4.20 a.m. Watches were synchronized and a final inspection made of the tank to ensure that everything was ready for the attack. Everything worked well, and it is certain from reports of prisoners that the enemy had no knowledge of our presence, previous to the attack.

We arrived at the jumping-off point just when the barrage commenced, and each tank at once got into its own sector in front of the infantry. At zero hour there was a very thick mist which made observation most difficult, and it was only by using my tank compass and following the barrage, that we were able to keep to our proper course. The mist lifted afterwards, about 6.45 a.m. Very little opposition was met with in the first phase of the attack, we had taken the enemy completely by surprise and they put up a poor fight. Whenever a tank was sighted they ran forward with their hands well up, and we passed them and allowed the infantry to deal with them. A few enemy machine guns kept on firing but they were soon silenced by running over them with the tank. Any of the gun teams who remained were dealt with effectively.

We reached our first objective at 7 a.m. and, after patrolling in front of the infantry until they had consolidated, we returned to our rallying point. Instructions were then received to proceed with two other tanks to assist the infantry in cleaning up the village of Bayonvillers. We entered the village, followed by the other tanks and infantry, and steered a zig-zag course through it, travelling down behind the houses and swinging round, then passing through a house and across the street, passing through a house on the other side and so on. This had the effect of bringing out any of the enemy who were hiding in the houses and they immediately surrendered. There was little resistance met with in this village and a good number of prisoners were rounded up and afterwards handed over to the infantry for disposal. We patrolled the village until the infantry commander informed us that the assistance of *Barrhead* was no longer required. We then set off for Harbonnières. On arrival there we found other tanks of the battalion cleaning up the village; they had also captured an enemy train full of reinforcements. After seeing that the village was cleared of the enemy, all the tanks returned to the rallying point.

TANKS AND TRENCHES

AMIENS

A Mark V of 2nd (B) Battalion approaching a sunken road at the time of Amiens.

It was a good day's work and the crews were in excellent spirits, although somewhat exhausted, having been in the tanks for nearly sixteen hours. *Barrhead* was in splendid condition and gave no trouble whatever during this, its first action. That night we again moved and took up a new position ready for further events. We arrived about 2 a.m. and slept in or near our tanks where we could make ourselves most comfortable. During the morning [9 August] orders were received to attack with the infantry, the starting point being to the south of Harbonnières. The approach march was over open country and in view of the enemy observation balloons. While waiting for the infantry to come up a number of shells dropped in the vicinity of the tanks but luckily they did no damage.

The attack commenced at 1.30 p.m. Strong opposition was met with from machine guns, anti-tank guns, artillery and bombing aeroplanes. The machine guns were soon silenced, *Barrhead's* six-pounder guns opened fire on some splendid targets and her machine guns poured forth a leaden hail of bullets on the Germans who were seen running in all directions. Pushing ahead and getting nearer the objective, the artillery fire became very heavy; shells kept bursting around *Barrhead* so the driver steered a zig-zag course to avoid them and meanwhile the gunmen kept up a heavy fire. At this time one of the crew was wounded, and while the NCO was examining his wounds, the tank was hit by a shell. The concussion from this shell threw the crew all over the tank and filled it with suffocating fumes. I got four of the crew outside and placed them at the rear of the tank as they were all wounded. On re-entering the tank to ascertain what had happened to the other two members of my crew I found them both dead. The shell, which must have been a large high explosive, had hit the tank in front of the right-hand sponson and burst inside, wrecking the cylinders of the engine.

After dressing the wounded men I sent three of them to the nearest dressing station and went in search of a stretcher for the other man whose wounds prevented him from walking. While I was bringing the stretcher the tank was again hit and burst into flames. When I returned I found that *Barrhead* was a blazing furnace and the ammunition going off like a machine-gun firing. The seriously wounded member of my crew has since died of his wounds in hospital.

The tank's position was near a hospital, midway between Vauvillers and Rosières, and I expect that it has since been salvaged and brought back to workshops where many of its parts may have been used to repair other tanks. Thus ended the career of *Barrhead*, and the loss of such a reliable tank is very

Another 2nd Battalion Mark V, knocked out near Bayonvillers on 8 August.

regrettable. It did splendid work on both days of the attack and was instrumental in capturing at least ten enemy machine guns and about two hundred prisoners. When one considers the number of lives of our own infantry that were saved by this tank, owing to its valuable assistance in subduing the enemy's fire and overcoming his resistance, the existence of *Barrhead* was well justified and the initial expense of its construction more than ten times repaid.

Signed 'Tank Commander' in the field, 10 August 1918

13TH BATTALION, 8 AUGUST 1918

B and C Companies of the 13th Battalion were to work in the northern sector of the Australian front. Here the 3rd Australian Division was entrusted with the capture of the first objective at an average depth of 4,000 yards, the 4th Australian Division being ordered to pass through them in the second phase. The general scheme of the opening assault was on the lines already made familiar on a smaller scale at Hamel. Tanks catching up their infantry were to follow an artillery barrage organized in depth, but moving at a faster rate than that employed in July; the rates of advance for each hundred yards being, on the start line three minutes, then two minutes to 200 yards, three minutes for the next 800 yards, then one minute up to the protective barrage 400 yards beyond the first objective. Smoke was only to be used in the first short standing barrage and in the protective barrage. In the second phase no barrage was to be employed, but guns moving forward would engage known battery positions; the RAF would drop smoke bombs to screen villages held by the enemy. As before, air protection was arranged for tanks moving up to the start line and when about to attack.

Col. Lyon and his company commanders discussed the plans with the divisional and brigade staffs with whom they were working. The other officers met and arranged schemes with the battalion and company commanders of the infantry, with many of whom they were already well acquainted. Tanks displayed on a painted board the colours of their own infantry, of whom one NCO stayed with each crew and rode as an observer in the tank on the day of battle. It may here be noted that these Australians were of the greatest use in keeping touch with the infantry and returned to their units with a largely enhanced opinion of the courage and endurance of the Tank Corps personnel. All the officers concerned carried out personal reconnaissance of their sectors, the parties so engaged being limited to a maximum of three at one time to avoid all display of abnormal movement. Much valuable information was also gained from air photographs issued by the Australian staff.

B and C Companies left their assembly point at Hamelet on the night of

7 August, and were all in position on their start line by midnight, except two tanks of B Company which were delayed by mechanical troubles, but were brought up by the company engineer in time for the attack. C Company, on the left, lay on the north side of Hamel village, while B Company, on the right, had two sections on either side of Vaire Wood: thus they occupied as start points positions which they had won by their former success. Here tanks were filled up with petrol and tapes laid to the infantry start lines.

Col. Lyon established his advanced headquarters behind Vaire Wood before the start; this was moved up behind the advance and opened later in Cerisy valley after its capture. Company commanders had their headquarters, B with the 9th and C with the 11th Australian Brigades. The ground was drying up after several days of rain and was in fine condition for tank operations. On the morning of the action a dense mist prevailed, making objects invisible at a distance of ten yards. This started to lift at 6.30 a.m., and from 7.30 a.m. visibility rapidly improved. All tanks started, and at zero, 4.20 a.m., with one appalling crash, the barrage fell. The most pronounced factor in this first phase of the attack was the mist. Compasses had been issued to the tanks of the 13th Battalion, but fittings for installing them had not arrived in time. In some cases

A female tank, fitted with the wider tracks, makes short work of a roadblock near Bayonvillers. It is carrying a small fascine and parts of a trench bridge.

improvised fittings were devised, while other tank commanders preferred to leave their tanks and use their own prismatics to maintain direction.

In these ways the tanks not only held their own course but also guided their infantry to the objective. A number of tanks were ditched from inability to see the ground in front of them; as against this disadvantage the moral effect upon the enemy of tanks emerging upon them from the mist was enormous, and the first objective was won with comparative ease. The tanks, having established their infantry, rallied back to the Cerisy valley behind them. Several incidents of interest had occurred in this period. One tank was disabled near Accroche Wood by running over a land mine, the first experience in the battalion of this form of anti-tank defence. One tank was of service in keeping touch between two companies of infantry who had become widely separated, until the gap in the line could be closed. A large number of machine guns had been run over and knocked out and prisoners surrendered freely. One officer, in need of labour to dig out his ditched tank, collected a gang of Saxons and kept them working until the tank was free; an intelligent prisoner pointed out a supply of German shovels for the purpose.

The second phase of the attack, which started four hours after zero, was very different from the first. The mist which had hampered, but concealed, the Allies' approach had now given way to brilliant sunshine. The enemy had ample warning of the battle and had time to station artillery and machine-gunners to meet the advance. In these conditions resistance stiffened. B and C Companies, having been in the first wave of the early attack, were now given a different role. One section of C Company, three tanks under Capt Fletcher, was specially detailed for mopping up the villages of Cerisy and Morcourt on the river edge in conjunction with tanks of the 8th Battalion. All the remainder were to form a supporting wave to the 8th Battalion, which took up the advance from this point, A Company with the 2nd Battalion working on its right. The objective for this stage was roughly the old Amiens defence line, which lay on the high ground east of Morcourt gully. It may be added that though this was regarded as the final objective, a further advance to an outpost line was intended, the infantry machine-gunners for this purpose being brought up according to plan in Mark V★ tanks, the Trojan horses of the Corps. In practice these gunners became travel sick and preferred to march outside. Further, the heavy tanks having broken the resistance, the Whippets, armoured cars and cavalry were to dash through and exploit the opening.

A Company started from their billets at Aubigny at 3.15 a.m., and were passing through the field artillery lines when the first crash of the barrage announced the opening of the attack. Thus the forward movement to their assembly points on the north and south sides of Warfusee was made not only through the dense mist of the early morning but also through the somewhat severe shell fire of the enemy's heavy batteries. The untiring efforts of 2/Lt H.H. Fletcher, the company engineer, were largely responsible for the success of this approach march. The role of this company, operating with their old friends the 8th Brigade of the 5th Australian Division, was to attack, following the line of the main road through Warfusee, their right section skirting the village of Bayonvillers. After reaching the final objective, they were to cooperate in the capture of Harbonnières. On the completion of this task, all tanks were to rally to their own battalion in Cerisy valley. Maj. Pape's eleven tanks left their assembly point shortly after 8 a.m., deployed in front of the infantry, and at 8.20 a.m., followed at a distance of about 200 yards by their Australians, started on their attack. The ground in this sector beyond Warfusee was level, rising at a slight slope towards a crossroads lined with trees. Behind this screen three German batteries were established and their guns commanded the approach over open sights. Six tanks of the company were knocked out almost in one line in front of this position. The casualties were severe, but nothing daunted, the survivors of the crews left their tanks and with their Hotchkiss guns attacked the artillery. 2/Lt Plews continued to move forward against these guns in spite of

A knocked-out Mark V near an advanced dressing station in the Warfusee-Abancourt area on 8 August 1918.

two direct hits on his tank, while that of 2/Lt Challis received three hits without being brought to a standstill. These officers were thus able to approach nearer than the rest to the hostile guns and, when finally knocked out, attacked the gunners on foot at the head of their crews. In this gallant fashion the batteries were captured and the advance enabled to continue. The five surviving tanks, three from Capt Black's section and two from Capt Hawkins', supported by the second wave, pressed forward towards the final objective. On the edge of Morcourt gully one of Capt Black's tanks was hit by a heavy shell in front. The driver and NCO in charge were both killed and the tank, completely out of control, plunged blazing down the ravine. L/Cpl Whiles, with great bravery, extricated the survivors and made repeated efforts, first to extinguish the flames and, when this was impossible, to remove the driver and tank commander, the ammunition exploding round him during the attempt.

The tanks of Capt Hawkins' section, commanded by 2/Lt Gray and Sgt Child, having reached their objective, turned towards Harbonnières and, entering this village from the east, were of assistance to Col. Bryce of the 2nd Battalion in suppressing a machine-gun nest which was holding him up while on his way to raise the Australian flag in the village. Later they returned to the Morcourt gully and were sent back by Maj. Pape to the rallying point in Cerisy,

Further north the other companies of the 13th were meanwhile advancing over undulating ground; the method of attack had been adapted to suit the conditions. Leaving the infantry established on a crest, tanks would go forward across the valley, maintaining fire on isolated machine-gun posts, and gain positions on the forward crest. In all cases this induced the enemy to give themselves up and enabled the infantry to advance to the next crest. On the right of this sector B Company, who, due to casualties in the first wave, were soon fighting in the front line, quickly placed their infantry in their final objective north of the main road. C Company on the left had more trouble. A field gun placed on the high ground across the river near Chipilly was in a position to enfilade the advance and knocked out three tanks soon after they passed the first infantry objective. This caused a withdrawal by the infantry. By noon, however, the remaining tanks had placed their infantry in the required positions and all active opposition had ceased. Throughout the operation there was abundant evidence of the hasty retreat of the enemy. In the gully south-east of Maucourt a transport park, complete with wagons and harness was left behind, and at the southern end of the same gully a field canteen was found well stocked with light wines and German beer.

In these two companies many officers and men distinguished themselves and their battalion. Capt Baker and Capt Hill, section commanders under Maj. Griffin, received special mention for fearless leading under fire. 2/Lt Gill not

Australian troops with a Mark V★ female tank of 15th (0) Battalion near Abancourt.

only displayed conspicuous gallantry in handling his tank and accounting for many enemy machine guns, but also, finding another tank set alight, got out to assist it and removed the wounded officer to shelter under heavy fire. 2/Lt Innes drove into a nest of machine guns in front of the objective. At this point the engine broke down and he became a target for the guns from all directions. Engaging the enemy with his own guns, he eventually succeeded in making a temporary repair, put all the enemy guns out of action and brought his tank back to the rallying point. The 13th Battalion returned to rally and refill in the Cerisy valley. Only three supply tanks attached to the battalion had succeeded in getting through to the rallying point, but these were sufficient to equip the survivors. A mobile dump formed by the battalion from borrowed wagons proved on this occasion to be more reliable than the Mark IV supply tank. On the evening of the 8th the position in the battalion was; eight tanks fit for action; eighteen hit and disabled by enemy fire, of which ten remained in the field. Two were ditched and not yet extricated, and eight were mechanically unfit, four of these being made ready during the night. One effective company therefore remained out of the original three. Among the personnel, five other ranks had been killed, nine officers and twenty-nine other ranks wounded, and

Tanks of 10th (J) Battalion temporarily camouflaged as they wait to start the second stage of the attack near Albert on 8 August.

two officers and four other ranks, though slightly wounded, remained at duty. Five other ranks were reported missing.

On 9 August the Australian Corps further advanced its line, but the 13th Battalion, engaged in refitting injured tanks and affording such rest as could be given to its exhausted crews, took no part in the fighting of that day. Eight tanks had moved on the evening of 8 August to Bayonvillers and four more, made ready for action, joined them there on the morning of the 9th to form a composite company for future operation under the command of Maj. Griffin, of whose own company seven tanks were present, with two of A Company and three from C.

On 10 August this company took part in an operation with the Canadian Corps who were advancing south of the Villers-Bretonneux to Chaulnes railway. The plan for this day was to continue the advance with the 4th Canadian Division on the left and the 32nd Division on the right. At the same time the Australian Corps was to attack and form a defensive flank to the north. The final objective for the Canadians was a line running from Hattencourt, through Hallu, to the railway junction south of Chaulnes.

The first intimation that the 13th Battalion was to be employed was received by wire at 12.15 a.m., but no information was then available either of the plan of attack or of the situation of the 4th Canadian Division; it was only known that the 13th Battalion would come under orders of the 4th Tank Brigade. Col. Lyon went to the 4th Brigade headquarters with Capt Boyd Rochfort of the Tank Corps Headquarters, but could get no information of the scheme of attack. Eventually he was able to discover the whereabouts of the Canadian 4th Division and from them ascertained the nature of the operation and the brigade with which the tanks of the 13th were to work. It was then 6.30 a.m. and orders were at once issued to the composite company at Bayonvillers to move to a point on the railway line at Rosières.

The company had no maps of this sector at the time and did not know the ground to the south of them. Capt J. Stewart, a section commander of the company, produced a small-scale German map which had been captured on the 8th, and with this as their sole guide they started at 7 a.m. All tanks were in position by 8.52 a.m., having covered a distance of 10,000 yards in under two hours. Here maps were issued by Maj. Griffin, who had obtained them from a Canadian staff officer whom he had stopped on the road, and section and tank commanders held a hurried consultation with the officers of the left attacking battalion.

Each tank brought with it to the start line sufficient petrol to fill up for the action. A supply tank was sent from Bayonvillers to the rallying point but broke down on the way, and a mobile dump which should have arrived in lorries from the 5th Tank Brigade did not get through.

The attack was timed for 10.15 a.m. Thus, a new phase in tank tactics was here attempted; tanks approaching by daylight and attacking in full view of the enemy. The long, straggling township of Rosières lay between the tanks and their infantry start lines, and made it necessary for sections to move forward in single file through the northern end before deploying southwards in front of their infantry. The special function of the tanks was to mop up the villages of Maucourt, Chilly and Hallu, and then to work forward to the final objective. Information was precise that the high ground of Lihons across the railway boundary on the north was already in Australian hands. But as the position was somewhat obscure, one section, that of Capt Hill, was detailed to protect the left flank of the attack. Lt Thomas was to capture Maucourt, Capt Stewart Chilly and Capt Willard Hallu. These were small villages which had been completely devastated in 1916.

All tanks started at zero. There was no barrage and the shelling of the villages by Allied artillery was slight. The resistance of the enemy was much greater than that encountered on 8 August. About 500 yards east of Rosières, at a point much nearer than had been expected, strong enemy machine-gun posts opened fire on the tanks and had to be disposed of before the deployment was complete.

Mark Vs, sporting their unditching beams, moving forward in column on 10 August.

Section commanders continued to guide their tanks on foot to the point of deployment, as lack of preliminary reconnaissance made this essential.

The going for the first 1,500 yards was good, but from that point the old trench system of 1916 had to be crossed. Several lines of old trenches, widened by use and weather and screened from view by luxuriant undergrowth, made driving difficult and accounted for the ditching of some tanks. Seven tanks reached their final objectives and established their infantry. The cooperation between tanks and infantry was far from good. The Canadians had no experience with tanks, and to the tank crews, accustomed to the dashing enterprise of the Australian Corps, seemed slow to avail themselves of the opportunities of advance which the tanks made. The infantry, on the other hand, were of the opinion that the tanks were too fast and kept too far ahead of them. That the tanks did most effective work and saved many casualties by destroying machine guns was freely admitted. What was lacking was the mutual understanding gained by previous practice. One example of this can be shown in the following experience. 2/Lt Fraser found that his infantry were held up by a number of machine-gun nests, and went forward some 600 yards to deal with them. In one of the old Somme trenches he became ditched and was immediately surrounded by the enemy who concentrated all available machine-guns – over twenty in number – on his tank, the sides of which were riddled with armour-piercing bullets. He fought his tank until all his Hotchkiss guns were out of action and all his crew wounded, his own infantry still remaining far behind. The enemy approached and called upon him to surrender, but he continued to hold them off with his revolver. After three-quarters of an hour the infantry moved forward and the remaining machine guns fell easily into their hands.

2/Lt Litchfield received a direct hit on his tank from an anti-tank gun. To make a temporary repair it was necessary to climb out under fire to the top of the tank. This officer and one of his crew worked on top of the tank in full view of the enemy and succeeded in making so good a repair that the tank later returned to the rallying point under its own power. 2/Lt Gray, who had driven into Harbonnières on 8 August, again displayed great determination. Coming under fire from a battery of guns, he received a direct hit on his tank, but being able still to move he made for the flank of this battery in the hope of enfilading it. A second hit killed one of his crew and wounded two others, but he continued to advance until a third hit brought his tank to a standstill. With a number of tanks disabled and ditched, the demands on the services of the

A Mark IV supply tank leads a Mark V★ female tank through a captured village.

technical staff were great, and both 2/Lt Kermode, the company engineer, and Mechanist Staff Sergeant Dobson, on several occasions advanced under fire to the assistance of stranded tanks, and with great skill and daring got them going again.

On the left flank the section under Capt Hill, detailed to watch the ground across the railway, soon found that the suspicion entertained of the Lihons ridge was well founded, as machine guns from this sector opened on the advancing Canadians from the Australian area. 2/Lt Spencer, the company reconnaissance officer, went forward on his own initiative and brought back valuable information as to the position, with the result that Capt Hill sent one of his tanks over the brigade boundary to deal with this situation, the tank engaging targets to the north and north-east, doing great execution until it became ditched in an old trench of the 1916 system. Had more petrol been available, more tanks might usefully have been sent from the rallying point to clear up this sector.

The tanks that could move rallied back to Rosières and thence drove to their starting point at Bayonvillers, which they reached with petrol quite exhausted, having covered since the morning a distance of over 35,000 yards. Five tanks remained in the field, three disabled by artillery fire while on the move, one set on fire by bombs while stationary and one ditched beyond hope of recovery.

17TH BATTALION AT BUCQUOY

On the night of 20 August no fewer than 120 tanks were concentrated on a four-mile front, with Bucquoy as its centre. The 3rd (Light) Tank Battalion was detailed as a mobile force to exploit any success and break through, if possible, up to and across the Bapaume–Arras road. Eight armoured cars of A Company, 17th Battalion, were attached to this battalion. Their orders were to get as quickly as possible across the broken country onto the good roads, do as much damage as they could in the rear of the enemy, and especially maintain communication with the Whippets of the 3rd Battalion up to and along the Arras–Bapaume road. To the north of this attack, which was allotted to X Corps, VI Corps was operating. In this area the 6th (Light) Battalion had a similar role to the 3rd. To it were attached two sections of B Company, 17th Battalion under Maj. Boucher. The only practical approach was by way of the road leaving the Arras-Doullens highway south of Bavincourt, running through Bienvilliers and Bucquoy, and crossing the railway at Achiet into the northeastern corner of Bapaume. Cars were therefore concentrated on the night of 20th–21st at Bienvilliers, with orders to move off at dawn. When the good roads

An oblique view of the battlefield near Bucquoy, looking towards Achiet le Petit.

were reached, B Company was to turn northwards and get in touch with the 6th Battalion, while A Company continued towards Bapaume.

Companies got along without adventure to the entrance to Bucquoy, where the road ran into a small cutting, in which a large crater had been blown by the enemy. The Whippets made a path around it and the cars were hauled over, one at a time, with drag ropes, pioneer parties working on the roads. The sections of cars were all on hard roads in the enemy's lines two hours after they left Bienvilliers.

By this time it was light, but a dense mist enveloped the battlefields, making it impossible to travel at any speed, owing to the danger of running into shell holes and other obstacles on the road. The Allied barrage was too heavy to penetrate, so at first movements were slow. The cars reached Achiet le Petit at 8.25 a.m., ahead of their infantry, and engaged the enemy occupying the ruins of the village, affording valuable covering fire to assaulting troops. As the mist was becoming thicker than ever and there was no sign of the Whippets, the cars determined to get through to Achiet le Grand. The leading car of B Company

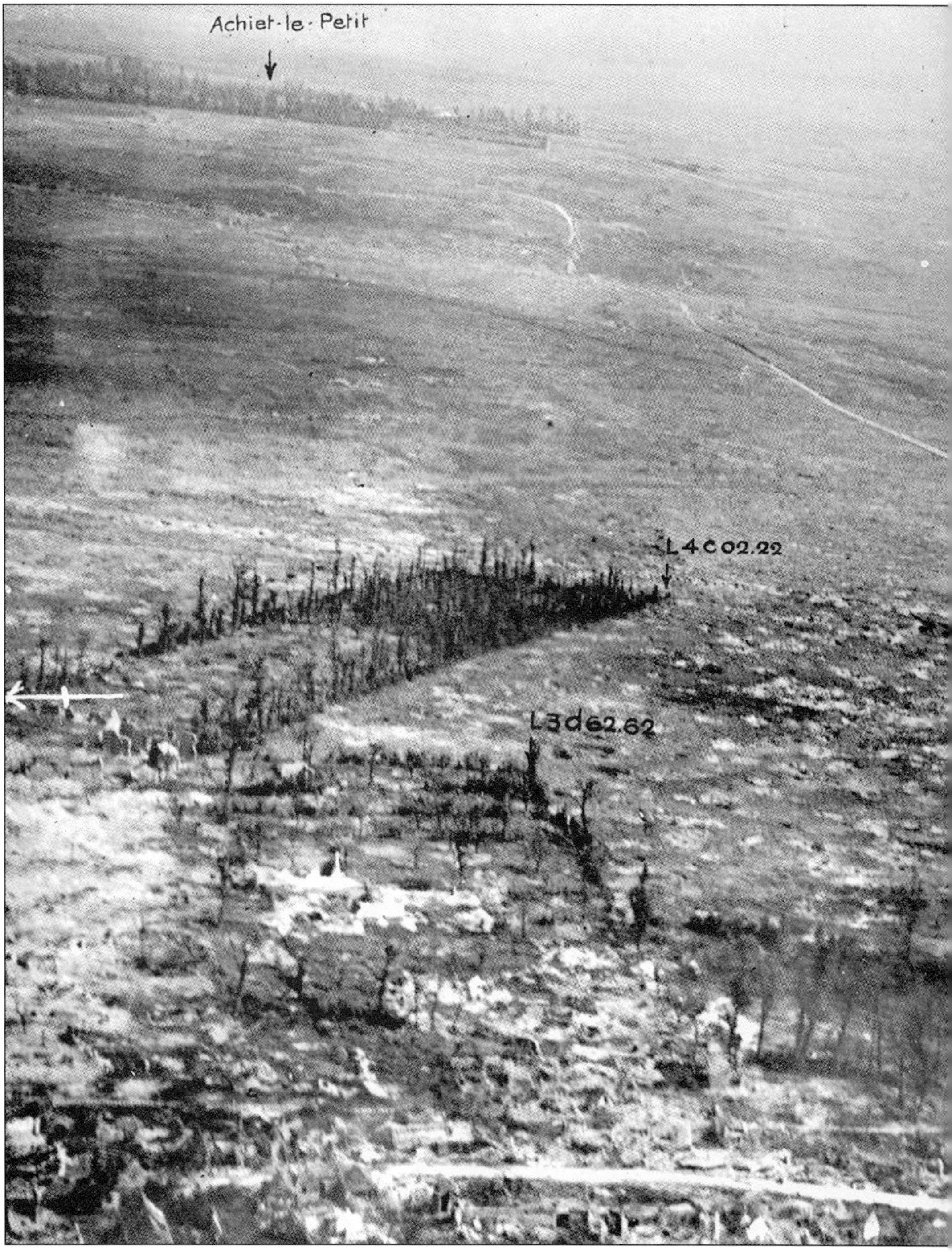
Achiet-le-Petit
L4c02.22
L3d62.62

L3d 55.10

L9b 90.93

5910.108.

The burnt-out wreck of Lt Herd's Austin on the road near Achiet le Petit.

took the wrong turning in the mist and ran into the sunken road north-west of Achiet le Petit, followed by two other B Company cars. The enemy had guns trained on the cutting. The first car sustained a direct hit. The second was hit too, sheared a key in the back wheel and ran away down the incline, hit the bank and burst into flames. The third car ran into the ditch, whence it was rescued later by a Whippet which suddenly appeared out of the fog. This was the first and last that was seen of the 3rd Battalion after the beginning of the action.

The remaining cars returned in search of the right road. They found their infantry held up outside Achiet le Petit so the cars patrolled the village streets while the infantry cleared out the enemy that was putting up a defence from the houses. By the time the Achiet le Grand road was found, valuable time had been lost. The barrage had ceased, the enemy was concentrating fire on the road, and the shell holes in it made it impassable for cars unassisted by towing tanks. The Allied infantry could not get past the outskirts of the village. Two cars of B Company had been hit and the other six were out of action through mechanical defects. The officer commanding A Company sent one of his sections along the northern road towards Courcelles to gain touch with the 6th Battalion, but the road was impassable. One section operated down the Achiet le Petit-Miraumont road as far as the railway embankment, where some enemy machine-gunners were holding up the infantry. Under the covering fire of the armoured cars the infantry were able to advance and obtain a footing on the railway embankment, which developed into the subsequent withdrawal of the enemy from the whole line of the railway to Achiet le Grand. After this there was no purpose for the cars to remain and they were all withdrawn at 2 p.m.

Two days were given for refitting the battalion. Those two days were taken up in the battle in carrying the line forward to within three miles of Bapaume and clearing the enemy from the old line through Achiet le Grand. On the morning of 24 August a general attack started from the Scarpe to the Somme. The armoured cars were attached to the New Zealand Division, to operate down the Achiet-Bapaume road and exploit successes, A Company south of a line drawn east and west through Bienvilliers and B Company north of it. A Company left Achiet le Petit, where the battalion lay for the night, two hours after zero to raid Grevillers and Avesnes, but was stopped by shell fire. B Company was more successful. Two sections went by way of Achiet, Bihcourt and Sapignies to the Arras–Bapaume road and then turned down towards Bapaume. The two woods just to the south of Favreuil, known as Monument Wood, had escaped destruction in the retreat. They were full of machine guns and trench mortars. So was the cemetery just north of the city. These points were effectively engaged by the armoured cars running down the road to within a short distance of the position, firing a few belts of machine-gun fire and then withdrawing. The cars finally returned, one with a broken dumb iron, one with defective steering, and all well-marked with machine-gun bullets. Reports had previously been sent back by pigeon, which materially helped to clear up the situation. Later in the day, as Monument Wood was still giving trouble, a section of A Company was sent to deal with it. Going by way of Bienvilliers and the crossroads at Favreuil, they penetrated right into the northern part of the town, took on numerous machine guns and a mortar battery with effect, and returned without casualties.

That little piece of road from the monument to the cemetery gave a great deal of trouble. It was very strongly defended by German tanks, in addition to machine guns and trench mortars. A railway ran by the roadside and a large ammunition dump had been formed there. It was not occupied by Allied troops until the 25th, when twelve heavy tanks assisted at the taking of it and even they suffered considerable loss, several tanks being put out of action near Monument Wood, where they remained derelict for some time. Yet, twenty-four hours before it fell into Allied hands, armoured cars of the 17th Battalion were patrolling freely down that section of road and returning unscathed, although they were continually engaged by enemy machine guns.

3RD BATTALION, 29 AUGUST 1918

I have the honour to submit the following report in connection with the action of one section of Whippets, 3rd (Light) Tank Battalion, under the command of Lt C.H. Sewell on the afternoon of 29 August 1918, east of Favreuil, and to recommend the act of Lt Sewell as worthy of a posthumous award for extreme gallantry and courage in action under heavy shell and machine-gun fire.

At about 2 p.m. on the afternoon of 29 August, Whippets of the 3rd (Light) Tank Battalion reached the quarry at map reference H14 d43. Acting under instructions received from the New Zealand Division, one section of Whippets under Lt Sewell was ordered to clear up the situation on the front of the 3rd New Zealand Rifle Brigade before Fremicourt and the Bapaume–Cambrai road, where the infantry were reported to be held up by machine-gun fire.

On reaching the railway line in advance of our infantry, enemy batteries and machine guns opened heavy fire on the section. In manoeuvring to avoid the fire and to retain formation, car No. A233, commanded by Lt O.L. Rees-Williams, side-slipped into a deep shell crater and turned completely upside down, catching fire at the same time.

Lt Sewell in the leading Whippet (about 70 yards in advance), on seeing the plight of Lt Rees-Williams' car, immediately got out of his own Whippet and came to the rescue. Unaided with a shovel he dug an entrance to the door of

A Whippet from Lt Sewell's section.

the cab, which was firmly jammed and embedded in the side of the shell hole; forced the door open and liberated the crew. (The latter, under cover of darkness, later managed to escape and succeeded in regaining our infantry outpost lines.) Although the crew had, in the meantime, succeeded in extinguishing the fire, had it not been for Lt Sewell's prompt and gallant action the imprisoned crew might have been burnt to death as they were helpless to extricate themselves without outside assistance.

During the whole of this time the Whippets were being very heavily shelled and the ground swept by machine-gun fire at close range. On endeavouring to return to his own car Lt Sewell was unfortunately hit several times, his body being subsequently found lying beside that of his driver, Gnr Knox, also killed, just outside their tank which, at that time, was within short range of several machine-gun and infantry pits.

Lt O.L. Rees-Williams states in his report:

I would like to emphasize the gallant way in which Lt Sewell came to our assistance, although enemy machine-gunners swept the ground. Had it not been for his assistance I, and my crew, would have been unable to get out.

Signed Lt Col. Walker Bell, commanding 3rd (Light) Tank Battalion,
1 September 1918.

Lt Sewell was awarded a posthumous VC.

A Medium A Whippet in the ruins of Proyart, 23 August 1918.

CHAPTER EIGHT

The Hindenburg Line

The Battle of Amiens and the actions that followed took a heavy toll of Tank Corps resources in both men and machines. However, by the end of September some 230 British machines had been assembled for a major assault upon the Hindenburg Line positions south of Cambrai. As a defensive obstacle the Hindenburg Line was prodigious, especially where it intertwined with the Canal du Nord and St Quentin Canal. Behind it was the equally formidable Hindenburg Support Line and beyond that again the Hindenburg Reserve, or Beaurevoir Line. Mark V tanks used in this assault carried Cribs, a lightweight, skeletal version of the fascine, but the longer Mark V★ tanks did not need them. The attacks which finally broke through these defences proved the continued need for the slower, heavy tanks, but the opportunities they made were admirably exploited by the lighter Whippets and armoured cars.

The Mark V★ tank was essentially a Mark V lengthened by six feet amidships. The extra length gave it an improved trench-crossing ability, although it was much more difficult to steer, and the extra space inside was exploited to carry infantry machine-gunners to occupy captured positions. In practice, conditions inside the tanks were so grim to unacclimatized infantry, that they suffered considerably and were often too ill to fight.

6TH BATTALION, 1 SEPTEMBER 1918

On 1 September two tanks under 2/Lts Mosley and Avin, in support of 62nd Division, made an attack on a strongpoint in front of Vaulx-Vraucourt. These tanks met with intense machine-gun fire and for a time had to turn back, but eventually helped the infantry to their objectives. The tank commanded by Lt Mosley was penetrated by armour-piercing bullets and while destroying a machine-gun position by crushing, it became ditched and caught fire. The crew were all wounded. A fine piece of rescue work was effected by Pte Sidell, who brought back the driver (Pte Tacchi) a considerable distance under fire.

On the night of 1–2 September nine Whippets under Capt Strachan left Gomiecourt to attack in the direction of Lagnicourt. Owing to the pressure at which the tanks had been working for the past five weeks, little time had been

A column of Whippets trekking in the early-morning September mist.

available for overhauling, and as the tanks were running badly it was impossible to get them up in time for the operation. The CO, Lt Col. R.A. West, left camp early on the morning of the 2nd with two mounted orderlies. It was his intention to get up with the Whippets, before they went into action, by Lagnicourt. He went as far as the infantry on horseback in order to watch the progress of the battle and to ascertain when to send the tanks forward.

He arrived at the front line when the enemy was in the progress of delivering a strong local counterattack. The infantry battalion had suffered heavy officer casualties and its flanks were exposed. Realizing that there was a danger of the battalion's giving way, Col. West at once rode in front of them under extremely heavy machine-gun fire and rallied the men. In spite of the fact that the enemy were close up to him he took charge of the situation and detailed NCOs to replace officer casualties. He then rode up and down in front of the men, in face of certain death, encouraging all and shouting to them, 'Stick it men, and show them fight.' He was killed. His last words were, 'For God's sake put up a good fight.' For his heroic behaviour on that occasion Col. West was awarded the Victoria Cross. While with the battalion, within the short space of time between 8 August and 2 September, West gained the VC, bar to his DSO and MC.

Maj. W.O. Gibbs now assumed command of the battalion and immediately received instructions to send two Whippets to clear up the enemy machine guns in the trenches north of the Bois de Vaulx. These, under Capt Oke, Sgt Squires and Cpl Cossum, proceeded to a point just west of the St Leger-Vraucourt road, and, with two companies of the Suffolk Regiment, advanced and consolidated the line of the ridge over which passed the road from Noreuil to Lagnicourt. The operation lasted only half an hour and was a complete success, between fifty and sixty prisoners being brought in.

6TH BATTALION, 19 SEPTEMBER 1918

On 19 September preliminary movement orders were received from headquarters, 3rd Brigade for the battalion to be prepared to entrain at Bouquemaison on or about the 23rd, its probable destination being the Peronne area. The ramp and station approaches were examined in Bouquemaison and necessary arrangements made with the RTO. Work on tanks was pushed forward with all speed, there being several temporarily unfit awaiting the arrival of spares. The battalion was to entrain at Bouquemaison on the 22nd, proceed by rail to Tincourt, four miles east of Peronne, and park up north of the railway, Tincourt being then the railhead for the Peronne area.

Ten Whippets of C Company and six Whippets of A Company trekked to Bouquemaison station during the morning, a distance of approximately 1½ miles, parking up in the station yard to await the arrival of the train. This arrived on schedule and the tanks were entrained without difficulty, leaving at 2.30 p.m.

Meanwhile, an advance party had proceeded to Tincourt by road and a temporary camp site was selected at Bois du Buire, with tank park adjoining. A few tents were erected and arrangements made to meet the train and guide the tanks up. The first train from Bouquemaison arrived at Tincourt at 1 a.m. on the 23rd. Little difficulty was met in detraining, despite the use of a side ramp in lieu of the usual end-on type. Tanks were trekked to Bois du Buire, one mile north of Tincourt, and parked in the wood. The second train, consisting of the remaining Whippets (four of A Company, eleven of B Company and one of C Company) left Bouquemaison during the afternoon of the 23rd. Two Whippets were left at Neuvillette, one each of A and B Company, these being unfit for trekking owing to a lack of spares.

On the 23rd stores brought up on the first train were lorried during the morning to the camp site at Bois du Buire. During the afternoon a wire was received from 3rd Brigade to the effect that tanks were to concentrate to the south of the railway and not on the north side as previously instructed. A small copse about 2,000 yards south of Tincourt was therefore chosen as a camp site and tank park, and arrangements made to erect temporary shelters and to meet and guide the Whippets up.

The second tank train from Bouquemaison arrived at Tincourt about 5.30 p.m., the tanks being quickly detrained and trekked across country to the camp and tank park. Stores from the train were lorried up from the station and a few tents erected. Owing to the congestion of traffic, due to the heavy concentration of all arms in the area, and other tanks also arriving at Tincourt, it was deemed advisable to leave the tanks at Bois du Buire for a further 24 hours and trek them to the copse, south of the railway, on the following day. On the 24th the temporary camp was much improved, company lines being established and small cookhouses being built. Crews also did maintenance work on several defective tanks.

Excellent camouflage existed at the copse, tanks being lined up on the southern and eastern edges. Consequently crews were able to work on their buses under natural cover. During the afternoon the Whippets from the first tank train trekked from Bois du Buire through Tincourt to the new camp. No difficulties were met with en route.

Reconnaissance officers and section commanders commenced a general study and examination of the ground eastwards towards Hagricourt, Villeret and Le Verguier, this area being indicated as a possible sector for the battalion in the forthcoming operations. From the 25th to the 29th was a period of preparation and study of the ground in an easterly direction. Work on tanks was pushed forward and all were soon fit for action. Routes, lying-up points, dump sites, refilling points, railway crossings, etc. were all examined, arrangements being made jointly with 9th Battalion, as many portions of the route overlapped and could be used mutually. A suitable lying-up point was selected in the valley west of Grand Priol Woods, and routes from this point eastwards, towards the St Quentin Canal, were examined and checked. Third Tank Brigade, consisting of 5th, 6th and 9th Tank Battalions, was allotted to IX Corps from Army Reserve. Distinguishing signs were now painted on all Whippets, IX Corps' sign being a large red IX and the 32nd Division sign being four white dots in diamond formation.

On the 27th one company of nine tanks, under Capt Howell of A Company, moved up at 7 p.m. along the route previously arranged to a lying-up point one mile north of Le Verguier and approximately three miles east of the canal at Bellicourt, the Roisel-Montigny railway being crossed at a prepared, ramped crossing in order to avoid damage. B and C Companies were in Corps Reserve at the copse south of Tincourt.

On the 29th, Z Day, Battalion headquarters were established at dawn at the 32nd Divisional Advanced Headquarters at Canbrieres Woods, one mile south of Le Verguier, a line being granted on the divisional switchboard and an aeroplane dropping station established. Owing to heavy mist in the morning, no messages were received by aeroplane until 11 a.m.

Tanks of B and C Companies left Tincourt at dawn, arriving at the lying-up point about 10 a.m. The route previously used by A Company was followed and no difficulties met with. On receipt of orders, tanks moved off from their lying-up point at 11.45, arriving at Magny-la-Fosse at 2 p.m., where they got in touch with the 32nd Division. An attack was organized with the object of securing the Lehacourt Ridge, and at 4.45 four tanks, under Lt Sanders, moved forward with the Border Regiment. The attack was entirely successful and the tanks returned at 5.25 p.m.

A report came through that there was a gap in the Allied line south of the village of Joncourt and two tanks, with a company of Argylls, left at 6 p.m. to close it. At the same time four tanks were sent up the valley to Lehacourt Ridge to clear up some troublesome machine-gun posts. The tanks patrolled for some time in front of the infantry, silencing the machine guns, and returned to the rallying point at 8.15 p.m. The two tanks working with the Argylls were successful in helping to close up the gap in the line, but as they were about to rally a shell burst between the tracks of A389 and the tank could not be moved. Finally, eight tanks rallied south of Magny-la-Fosse at 8.30 p.m. A brigade rallying point was established in Springbok valley, 1,000 yards east of Magny-la-Fosse and 500 yards east of the canal. Tanks of B and C Company were moved about one mile eastwards towards the canal, lying up in the valley near Chakan-Grand Priol Woods for the night.

On the 30th orders were received from 3rd Brigade to the effect that 32nd Division was to attack the Beaurevoir-Masnieres Line on 1 October and OC 6th Battalion was to arrange details with GOC 32nd Division and be prepared to employ Whippets should a suitable opportunity occur. Tanks of A Company under Capt Howell cooperated with the 14th Infantry Brigade in the attack on Joncourt.

At 12.30 p.m. on the 30th OC A Company effected liaison with GOC 14th Infantry Brigade with a view to attacking Joncourt in conjunction with the 15th Lancashire Fusiliers. It was arranged for three tanks to move to a point 800 yards north-east of Magny-la-Fosse and from there proceed up the valley towards Joncourt, entering the village from the south and assisting the infantry, who were lying up west and south of the village. At 2.30 p.m. three tanks, under Capt Farrar, moved off to the point north-east of Magny, arriving there at 2.45. One tank was left here in reserve and the other two moved off to the attack at 3.30. On approaching the railway south of Joncourt, they came under heavy machine-gun and anti-tank fire. Lt Holloway's tank received three hits from an anti-tank gun and was put out of action. The second tank reached the outskirts of the village but, as no infantry followed, returned to try and pick them up. Failing to get in touch with the infantry, and with engines running badly, it returned to the valley. The reserve tank was then sent up to work right through the village but was knocked out by anti-tank fire just south of the railway at Joncourt.

Tanks of B and C Companies, under orders from the commanding officer, moved forward from Grand Priol Woods at 3 p.m. to the rallying point at Springbok valley, arriving without trouble, having followed A Company's tracks and crossed the canal south of Bellicourt. All tanks of this battalion were now concentrated at the brigade rallying point at Springbok valley.

13TH BATTALION, 23 SEPTEMBER 1918

After the operation of 23 August the companies had withdrawn, A to Aubigny, and B and C to Querrieu Wood. On 29 August the battalion moved to the neighbourhood of Villers-Bretonneux and entrained for transport to Boisleux au Mont near Arras. Here they came into reserve with the 3rd Army, which was then engaged in extending the successful advance against Bapaume. For some days the battalion, now with twenty-one tanks available, was in high hopes of taking a further share in the attack, and all ranks worked strenuously to fit the tanks for action. Actually they were not employed in the area, and remained in camp refitting tanks and training reinforcements until 20 September.

During this period a marked change had taken place in the general situation. The German Armies had withdrawn from the Lys salient, the battle of the Scarpe had resulted in the storming of the Drocourt–Queant Switch Line and nothing remained for the enemy but to establish its defence in the main Hindenburg Line. Against these new positions a further attack was now launched by the British Commander-in-Chief.

On 20 September the 13th Battalion moved by train from Boisleux to Tincourt, thus passing to the 4th Army area through Amiens, via Heilly and the familiar Rosières line, which was now open for traffic. Here in a wood near Tincourt were formed two composite companies under Maj. Maurice and Maj. Morrison which, on the night of the 22nd, moved forward to an assembly position near Leaf Wood for operations with IX Corps. A new method of approach march was now employed. The tanks were driven by skeleton crews and all the fighting men were withdrawn back to the camp by lorry, thus securing the longest possible rest before action.

The operation about to be undertaken was on the following lines. Between St Quentin and the village of Bantouzell the Hindenburg defence system was

Mark V★ tanks moving by rail in France. All have their sponson folded in and are sheeted down, but they have still attracted the attention of a group of local youngsters at a level crossing.

organized in depth, partly on the west, but mainly on the east side of the St Quentin Canal. Before an attack on the main system and the canal line could be undertaken, it was necessary to carry the outpost system in which the enemy showed every intention of a determined resistance. The function of IX Corps was to storm and secure the high ground north of Selency and east of Fresnoy, from which could be obtained observation and command of the main defences.

The Corps was to attack on a two-division front. At the same time the 46th Division were to cooperate on the left of the attack, while the 36th French Corps were to carry, on the right, Round Hill, Manchester Hill and the village of Francilly. Of the tanks of the 13th Battalion, B Company, under Maj. Maurice, with eight tanks was to work with the 6th Division on the right and C Company, twelve tanks under Maj. Morrison operated with the 1st Division on the left. It must be remembered that the operation was to further the advance made on the previous days, in which tanks had already been employed. There was, therefore, little hope of a surprise, the only factors likely to be unknown to the enemy being the time at which the blow would fall and the exact direction from which it might come. The Germans were systematically drenching the forward area with gas shells, and the tank assembly point had therefore to be fixed a considerable distance, from three to four miles, from the tank start lines. The time available for reconnaissance and liaison work was short, and the steps taken in these vital matters were confined to the senior officers, while tank commanders were preparing for the start.

The plan in detail from north to south was this. Of C Company, No. 3 Section, working with the Northants Regiment of 2nd Brigade, was to strike due east to seize the high ground south of Pontrouet, clearing woods and trench systems on the way. South of this two tanks of No. 5 Section were to operate with the Royal Sussex Regiment of the 2nd Brigade in the front line. Two more tanks were to follow 45 minutes later with a battalion of the King's Royal Rifles to mop up woods in which resistance might spring to life after the first wave had passed. No. 4 Section was to operate independently with the 3rd Brigade, working round Fresnoy village, clearing the cemetery and finally attacking Cornouillers Wood with two tanks from the east and two from the west. The general line of advance was, therefore, to the north-east. South of this again, the two sections of B Company were to attack in a south-easterly direction, with a starting point near Badger Copse. No. 1 Section, with the 16th Brigade, was to make for the trench system joining Dom Wood to the fortified post known as the Quadrilateral, while No. 2 Section was to attack the Quadrilateral itself.

Artillery cooperation by barrage fire and smoke was provided, and the RAF was to assist both by flights covering the approach of tanks and by dropping smoke or bombs on suspected points. Further, No. 1 Special Company, Royal Engineers, was to provide a smoke curtain to screen both the Quadrilateral in the first stages and the village of Selency south of this. There was thus an unusually heavy screen of smoke employed; concealment was to some extent to take the place of surprise in the attack. For the same reason, zero was fixed for the early hour, for tanks, of 5 a.m. A supply dump of twenty-two complete fills was formed at the rallying point, and a mobile dump on lorries near the same spot. Tanks brought up with them sufficient to refill before starting into action.

Both companies moved off on the final approach march about 8.30 a.m. To reach their position it was necessary to pass through the northern portion of the Great St Quentin Wood, where some delay was caused by overhead signal wires, which were constantly fouling the semaphore standards, and had to be carefully disengaged. Behind this wood the ground was under observation from the enemy by day, and was now continually searched with 5.9 shells, both HE and gas. In consequence, much of the march was made with doors closed and gas masks worn, and the crews suffered greatly from exhaustion and fumes. The tanks of B Company also came under heavy shell fire on reaching their start positions. It is possible that their presence was known or suspected, as a German plane twice dropped flares over Capt Bairstow's section. The moon was brilliant throughout the night and made perfect concealment impossible. It may be added that the statements of prisoners taken in this action show that the Germans were fully aware that an attack by tanks was coming and that they had made arrangements to meet them. These did not stop the tanks, save in one sector, and did not repulse the attack.

Both companies started up to time and preceded their infantry in the assault. The right section of B Company became the objective, at the start, of concentrated shell fire which inflicted two direct hits on one tank, and wounded the section leader, Capt Hill. The three remaining tanks made for the Quadrilateral. This was actually a pentagon system of trenches, enclosing fortified cottages, and backed towards the east by a high bank, which the enemy had tunnelled for the movement of troops and guns. Two tanks of the 2nd Battalion had been knocked out there on the previous day, and these had been reinforced with sandbags and were manned as machine-gun posts. All

A burning Mark V male tank near Bray.

three tanks penetrated the defences and inflicted heavy losses on the enemy, but there their success ended. One struck a landmine and was split in half, only one NCO and the infantry observer escaping alive. The second was hit twice and set on fire by anti-tank shells, the crew escaping with their Hotchkiss guns to join the infantry. The third (2/Lt Benson), attacking dugouts in the high bank, was ditched sideways and then repeatedly hit and set alight. The crew were forced to escape the flames and fell into the hands of the enemy. The infantry, deprived of tank assistance, reached the upper and lower corners of the Quadrilateral but were unable completely to master this strongpoint.

Meanwhile, the other sections of the company had passed through a severe fire, chiefly from woods on their left. They successfully engaged and silenced machine-gun posts in these, the centre tank also running over and crushing two machine-gun nests near the final objective. The right tank was hit, ditched and set on fire after proceeding 600 yards. The other two established their infantry with slight losses in the trench system which formed the final objective, but, finding this line enfiladed by a German field gun from Dom Wood, 2/Lt Barker made a bold attempt to silence it by approaching the wood. His tank was hit and the petrol ignited. On foot he then attacked the gun with Hotchkiss fire at short range, and silenced it by destroying the crew. The gun was subsequently captured. The remaining tank (2/Lt Finmore) had the singular good luck, having received two direct hits from the field gun, to remain mobile and ultimately rallied as the sole survivor of the tanks of this company.

In the northern sector C Company had reached their starting points by 4 a.m., with their crews much distressed by gas and suffering from petrol fumes. In three cases the entire crew were out of action from this cause, and in a fourth case a shell burst near the tank before starting and disabled most of the crew, the remainder being transferred to complete defective crews. There were thus seven tanks left to start in the first wave. These proved of great assistance to the infantry in reaching their objectives, but the casualties among the tanks were heavy. Three operating with the 3rd Brigade forced the garrison of Fresnoy to surrender and captured the fortified cemetery east of the village. Beyond this 2/Lt Millar's tank was hit and set on fire, two of the crew being wounded. The officer was killed in the open during a daring effort to save his guns. The remaining tanks of this section went forward to the final objective at Cornquillers Wood. On the left, Capt Maitland's section encountered stiff resistance from Pontrouet. However, he led his tank into action on foot and directed its fire against points that were holding up the infantry. His courage and resource enabled the advance to proceed, the enemy surrendering freely to the tanks. In the centre section 2/Lt Whyte, finding the infantry slow in the advance, repeatedly went forward and dealt with machine guns which were checking the assault, returning on each occasion to encourage his infantry forward. His tank was finally knocked out within a few yards of the objective, part of the petrol feed pipe being blown away. Having seen his infantry established, he rigged up a temporary feed and succeeded in saving his tank under heavy fire. For this purpose a petrol tin had to be filled from the main supply outside the tank. Ptes Hickman and Reilly volunteered to do this, and calmly filled a tin with a small hand pump while the tank was a target for all guns within range.

As a result of this action, the points of observation which formed the objectives were won. Even the Quadrilateral was outflanked on the left by the 1st Division, and commanded from the right by the French, who had made good Round Hill and Manchester Hill. The possession of these points was of great importance in the main attack upon the canal. But of the tanks employed, the losses were very heavy. Operating at short notice over unknown ground with infantry who had no experience of tank tactics, they became the targets for an enemy who was expecting their attack. That they met with any measure of success is a fine testimony to the gallantry and enterprise of the crews. Of C Company eight tanks returned or were towed to the rallying point. Of B Company, one only. Nine tanks remained in the field, still under enemy fire, and could not be saved for the present. Casualties among personnel were: Killed, one officer; wounded four officers and twenty-six other ranks. One officer and twelve other ranks were missing. Of these, 2/Lt Benson and his crew were ultimately repatriated, after having been prisoners of war, and the death in action of the remainder was proved by salvage parties. One officer casualty occurred on the approach march. 2/Lt Pilgrim was riding on the tank with his body half out of the front cab in order to direct his driver. While the tank was descending a steep bank the chain securing the unditching beam broke and the heavy beam slid forward, inflicting upon this young officer injuries from which he subsequently died.

1ST BATTALION, 27 SEPTEMBER 1918

On 20 September orders were received to move to Mannacourt and by the 23rd all tanks were in the tankodrome there. Ten tanks then arrived at Tincourt to be taken over by C Company, who were to move up to Blangy, but owing to the derailment of a train they were unable to complete their journey and their place had to be taken by B Company of 4th Battalion. Tanks were then prepared for action and reconnaissance of the forward area was carried out up to the 27th, on the evening of which the tanks moved to their deploying points. The battalion

THE HINDENBURG LINE

US infantry watch as Mark V tanks of 8th (H) Battalion move up to the Hindenburg Line, carrying their cribs. To the left one can just see a separate line of supply tanks advancing.

operated with the 30th American Division and by means of tape routes approached to just behind the front line.

At 5.30 a.m. on the 28th all the tanks went over to the attack, the object of which was to breach the Hindenburg Line and secure the tunnel entrance to the Canal de Torrens. A Company, consisting of twelve tanks, moved forward to the north of Bellicourt, while B Company worked south through Nauroy. The extremely heavy mist, combined with the dense smoke barrage, made the maintenance of direction a very difficult matter and the compasses in the tanks proved of immense value. Eight tanks of A Company were able to reach the Hindenburg Line, where they crushed a thick belt of wire and succeeded in silencing a large number of machine guns. They then went on to their final objective, but two received direct hits and two were ditched, only four arriving at the further end of the tunnel. Of B Company, seven cars made good progress and cleared much ground east of Bellicourt and north of Nauroy. During this operation two of their cars received direct hits and two had to stop owing to mechanical trouble and were burnt. Great success attended this operation against the enemy's strongest line of defence, though, had observation been better, much greater results would have been achieved.

Tanks with cribs, pitching like ships in a rough sea, move along the horizon behind a column of troops.

A very good action was fought by 2/Lt Hapgood's tank, which was ditched in the Hindenburg Line within 20 yards of the enemy. The enemy was strongly established at this point and directed very heavy fire onto the tank, with trench mortars, machine guns and even hand grenades. Notwithstanding this, Lt Hapgood held out for two days until the arrival of some Australian troops, who succeeded in dislodging the enemy. This officer and his crew then unditched the tank and proceeded to the rallying point.

The battalion rallied in the valley behind Hargicourt on the evening of the 29th and the next day salvage work and repairs to damaged tanks were put in hand.

301ST BATTALION, 29 SEPTEMBER–23 OCTOBER 1918

The 301st US Heavy Tank Battalion, equipped with Mark V tanks, left Wool for France on 24 August 1918, and was attached successively to the 4th and 2nd Tank Brigades. On 29 September the battalion supported the attack of the 27th and 30th American Divisions against the Hindenburg Line between Le Catelet and Bellicourt. The attack was unsuccessful and many misfortunes dogged the

THE HINDENBURG LINE

Said to be a genuine picture of tanks in action, this is reputed to be four Mark V tanks of the 301st Heavy Tank Battalion, US Army. Quite who might have taken such a photograph, under these conditions, is another matter.

tracks of the new battalion. An anti-tank minefield had been laid in the Maquincourt valley by the British forces as a defence against German tanks, and some of the unsuspecting American tanks were blown to pieces while making their way over them. Owing to the effective German artillery fire, the density of the smoke created by Allied barrage fire and the lack of cooperation, the heavy tanks were unable to make much headway and suffered many casualties.

The next action, on 8 October, proved a very different operation. In conjunction with 2nd American Corps, and between the 6th British Division (right) and 25th British Division (left), the 301st advanced to the enemy's lines at Brancourt. Two companies of the 6th (Whippet) Battalion were to assist in the exploitation. Preliminary preparations were thorough, the terrain was ideal and weather conditions favourable. Twenty out of the twenty-three tanks started and eleven reached their final objectives. This attack was continued on 17 October but the weather conditions were very unfavourable to tanks. From zero hour until noon there was a heavy mist and the drivers found that it was impossible to see where they were taking their machines. But in spite of this, and the fact that the River Selle divided them from the enemy, nineteen machines went into action after crossing the river on improvised bridges, and of these three reached their first objectives.

The last action of the heavy tanks took place on 23 October 1918, when three sections of the 301st Battalion were attached to the 2nd British Tank Brigade and placed at the disposal of the 6th British Division, which was to attack immediately south-east of Le Cateau towards Bois l'Evêque and Catillon. Contrary to established practice, zero hour was fixed for 1.20 a.m. in order to take advantage of the darkness for cover, surprise and moral effect. This departure from the normal attack at dawn proved successful, for the inevitable dense shelling at the concentration point was escaped. During the attack, however, the enemy freely used gas shells, necessitating the wearing of masks and thus hampering the tank crews. Each of the three sections advanced with three tanks, the fourth being held in reserve, and did splendid work in opening up the advance of the infantry. The tanks met with little opposition but were badly supported, or the infantry suffered heavy casualties from gas and were unable to keep pace with their advance. Eight of the nine tanks that took part in this action rallied the following morning. The only casualties suffered were five men slightly gassed.

In the words of Col. Fuller, 'The attack on this day was altogether a fitting conclusion to the brief but conspicuously gallant career of the 301st American Tank Battalion.' From the date of the Armistice until February 1919 the battalion remained attached to the British Tank Corps, reorganizing, equipping and holding extensive training in all tank subjects.

3RD BATTALION, 29 SEPTEMBER 1918

On receipt of the Australian divisional and 5th Tank Brigade orders with the artillery programme map, and all details having been decided upon, battalion orders for the operation were issued and, in accordance with the same, all companies left their lying-up places at 6 a.m. on the morning of 29 September and arrived behind the formations to which they were allotted and subsequently reached the Brown Line according to programme, without a hitch.

Ground mist and considerable mustard gas shelling were encountered during the approach march, to the discomfort of crews, but no serious cases of gassing developed until after the Whippets rallied, when it was found necessary to evacuate one officer and two other ranks to hospital. Several minor cases of gassing occurred, but they were not evacuated.

On reaching the Brown Line on the 3rd Divisional front about 9 a.m., the situation was found to be rather obscure. The Brown Line itself, that is the enemy front-line system, was under enemy machine-gun fire and there was no information available as to how far the American Division, who preceded the Australian Division, had got on. Consequently, the 3rd Australian Division did not launch their attack at 9 a.m. as intended.

A Company was proceeding alongside the road from Hagricourt when it encountered enemy machine-gun fire. Maj. Monk, commanding A Company, went ahead to ascertain the situation and learnt from various sources that the attack was held up in the neighbourhood of Quennemont Farm and Quennee Copse, and that the situation around Bony was obscure, but that Bony was believed still to be in enemy hands. Heavy tanks were observed advancing with the infantry and two were seen to receive direct hits. Enemy machine-gun fire was still active on the left and was causing considerable casualties to our troops. Maj. Monk ordered a Whippet tank to deal with same and the machine-gun crew surrendered to our infantry on the approach of the Whippet.

Information was received that enemy machine-guns in the vicinity of Quennemont Farm were holding up the advance and three Whippets under Capt O'Dowd were immediately detailed to deal with the situation. On reaching the points indicated, no machine guns could be located but the fire from this direction had ceased. Later the enemy holding these points surrendered to our infantry.

Hostile shelling had now increased considerably and Maj. Monk, learning from the officer commanding 17th (Armoured Car) Battalion that Bony was still in the enemy's hands, and that the trench system was impossible to negotiate, decided to withdraw his company to the crossroads near Malakoff Farm until the situation improved. Word was received from the Australian Brigade, who were holding the line, that a counterattack was expected and the company was held in readiness to repel any attack that might develop. Subsequently word was received that a further advance would not take place that day and Maj. Monk was ordered to withdraw his company to the rallying point near Hagricourt, where they arrived about 6.30 p.m.

B Company, under Maj. Way, who were working with 17th Battalion, proceeded to a rendezvous at the crossroads near Malakoff Farm, which they reached at 9.30 a.m. and where the armoured cars were to be met. A considerable amount of shell fire was encountered and also a certain amount of indirect machine-gun fire which was responsible for a number of casualties to men outside the tanks. On reaching the crossroads, armoured cars had not turned up and, after waiting half an hour, Maj. Way proceeded to get in touch with the situation and find, if possible, the whereabouts of the armoured cars.

Capt Saunders was left in command of the company and was ordered to take his tank and reconnoitre the road towards Bony. If he found it practicable he was to proceed towards the village with the rest of the company of tanks. Meanwhile, Maj. Way got in touch with the armoured cars near Hagricourt, where he was informed that the armoured cars had moved off, and he was instructed to push on with his tanks as soon as possible. On arrival back at the company it was found that the armoured cars had gone through towards Bony without communicating with the tanks but the Whippets followed on as rapidly as possible in their wake. At 11.15 a.m. Capt Saunders returned from his reconnoitring wounded and reported heavy machine-gun fire over the crest. His tank was taken over by 2/Lt Ridley.

The leading tanks, after crossing the crest, came under heavy machine-gun fire which they attempted to crush; they were, however, directly afterwards knocked out by enemy artillery. The majority of the armoured cars returned to south-east of the ridge, where they met the remainder of the Whippets and owing to the casualties it was decided not to advance further.

The tanks which had gone over the ridge were B25 Curmudgeon III, B26 Cynic III, B27 Crusty III and B28 Crab V. These were all knocked out by direct hits, burnt out, and the crews became casualties. About 6 p.m. Lt Ridley went forward with four men to the abandoned tanks to report on the possibility

A Whippet with spare petrol cans hanging off everywhere and even more lying on the tracks. It appears to have been knocked out since graffiti, claiming that the Germans captured it, has been partly erased on the cab side.

THE HINDENBURG LINE

of salvage and to leave guards on them. He was only able to reach two, and in doing so lost two of his men. He therefore withdrew the whole party, as further attempts at salvage were impossible owing to the heavy machine-gun and artillery fire. The remainder of this company were ordered to withdraw to the battalion rallying point, where they arrived about 7 p.m.

The 5th Australian Division advanced from the Brown Line at 8 a.m. C Company, under Maj. Scupham, followed at 9.15 a.m. and, finding it impossible to proceed by the side of the Red Road, owing to the ground being badly cut up with shell craters and the trench system too wide and deep, they had to travel part of the way on the road. Progress was somewhat delayed owing to mist which was very thick.

On arriving at a wood north-west of Bellicourt, indirect machine-gun fire was encountered, so the company halted and Maj. Scupham went forward to obtain some information about the situation. He gathered that the enemy were still holding out west of the Green Line and, on getting in touch with an

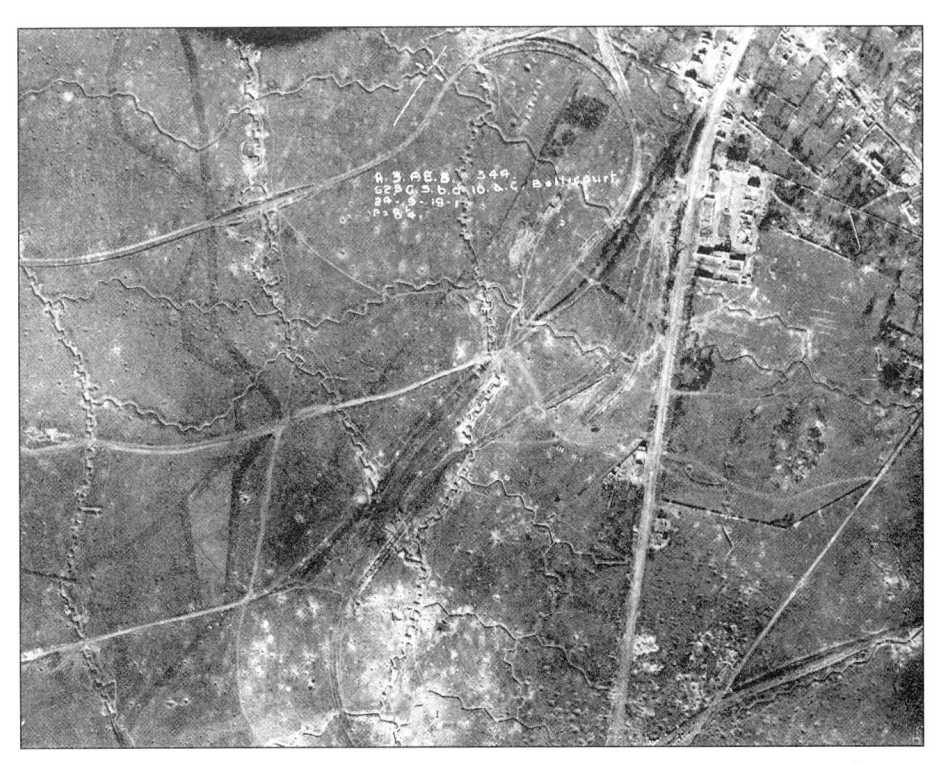

A vertical view showing the maze of trenches, wire and abandoned railway lines near Bellicourt, just beyond the Hindenburg Line.

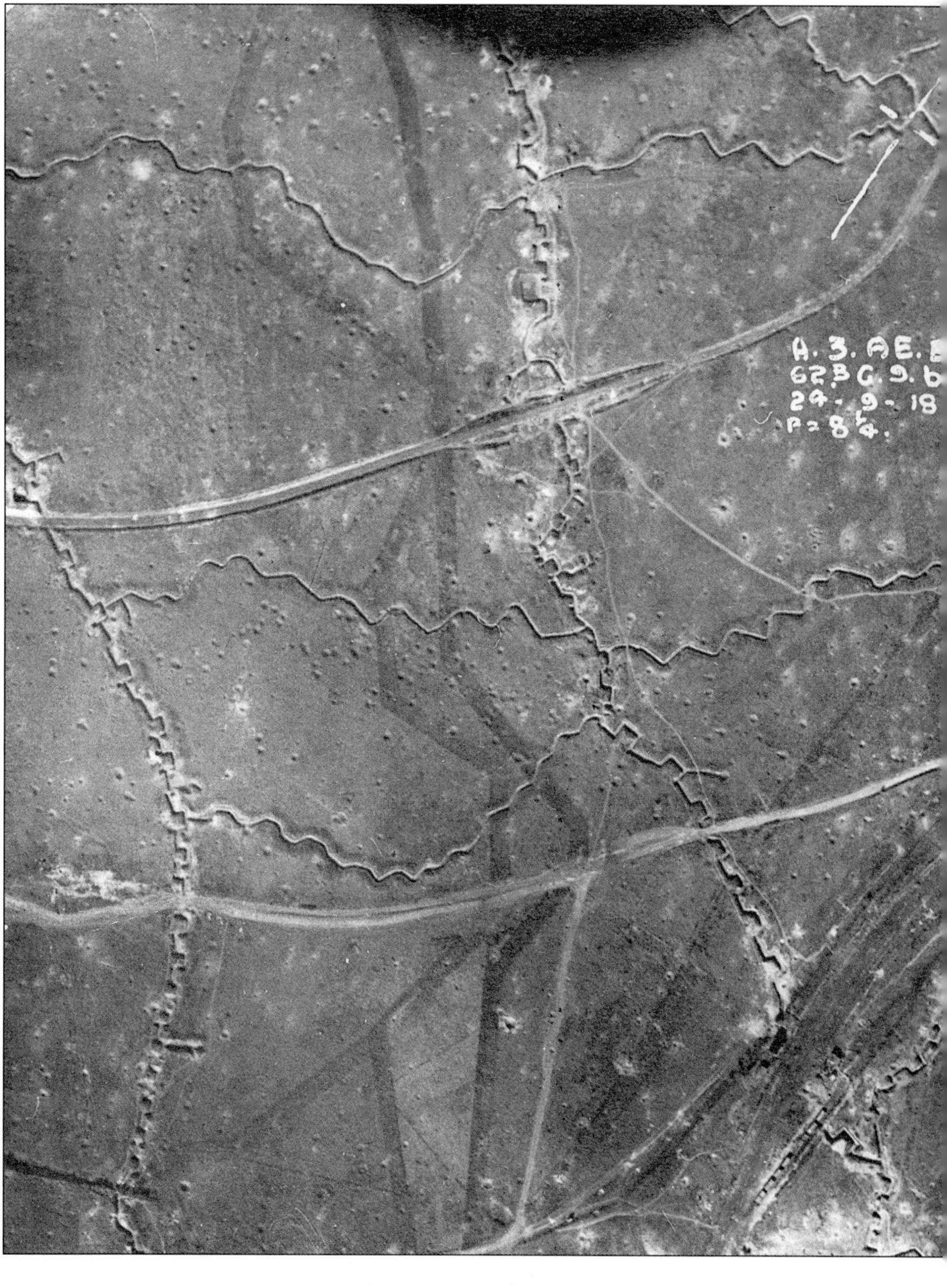
A. 3. AE. E
62.B G. 9. b
24 - 9 - 18
P = 8¼.

THE HINDENBURG LINE

Australian infantry battalion commander, ascertained that our infantry were in contact with the enemy; but no trace could be found of the American troops of the first wave. The infantry were moving forward and the infantry battalion commander said he would communicate with him later.

The Whippets were then taken off the road and moved into low ground north-west of Bellicourt. At 10.15 a.m., the fog having lifted, our infantry were seen advancing on the high ground west of Bellicourt. At 11 a.m. information was received that our infantry was held up by machine guns established in nests west of the Le Catelet–Nauroy Lines and required tanks to assist them. C Company commander at once detailed Capt Arnold, with four Whippet tanks, to push on through the infantry and deal with the machine-gun posts. On arrival at the canal bank he found five Mark V tanks, and the infantry commander told him not to go forward at once as an organized attack was taking place at 3 p.m. In the meantime the remainder of C Company moved up to the canal bank.

At 3 p.m. the infantry attacked with five Mark V tanks in front and eight Whippets in rear, Capt Arnold's section being on the left and Capt Archibald's section on the right. Their orders were to remain behind the infantry until the Le Catelet-Nauroy Line was crossed by the Mark V tanks and then cross over with the Whippets and move forward as rapidly as possible. Their objective was Estrées, which they were to encircle but not enter. The infantry objective was the Red Line.

On crossing the high ground immediately east of the canal all five Mark Vs were knocked out by direct hits. Two tanks of Capt Archibald's section were ditched in the Catelet Line due west of Estrées; one tank fell on its side, the other bellied. The remaining two tanks of this section, under Cpl Cousins and L/Cpl Kimberley, moved further down the trench and eventually crossed and fired into Nauroy Wood. The two tanks then moved north on the east side of the Le Catelet-Nauroy Line as far as Cabaret Wood Farm. They fired a number of rounds into the farm, which they cleared of the enemy, and then recrossed the trench and returned safely to the company rallying point south-west of Bellicourt.

Of Capt Arnold's section one tank was compelled to stop north of Bellicourt owing to engine trouble. The others reached the Catelet Line but could not find a crossing suitable so, after firing at the enemy in Cabaret Wood Farm, they returned to the company rallying point. It was then getting dark, and the remaining seven tanks of the company moved off to the battalion rallying point. On arrival Capt Arnold reported that his tank was immobile through engine trouble and had been left north of Bellicourt. The tank was subsequently brought in undamaged early the following morning together with the two

Whippets of Capt Archibald's section (which were unditched in the Catelet System) by Capt Archibald and Lt Cotton under enemy observation and heavy shell fire.

13TH BATTALION, 30 SEPTEMBER 1918

The Battalion rested their personnel at Tincourt until 29 September; by this date nine tanks had been made fit for action and these were collected at Templeux le Guerard, which lay to the west of Hagricourt and therefore opposite to that sector of the St Quentin Canal which, running through a tunnel between Hellicourt and Vendhuille, was practicable for tanks. The main attack upon the Hindenburg Line had already been successfully opened on the 27th by the 1st and 3rd Armies to the north in the direction of Cambrai; the 4th Army, after a preliminary bombardment for two days, attacked the covered portion of the canal on 29 September. On this day the nine tanks of 13th Battalion, formed into a composite company under Maj. Morritt, were in Corps Reserve, nine tanks of the 16th Battalion also being attached to Col. Lyon's

A Mark V★ male tank works its way through Beaucourt, as a group of prisoners carrying a stretcher make their way to the rear.

command. The failure of an advance by the American Corps on the first day had left the position east and west of the tunnel very obscure; enemy posts were known to be still holding out on the west side, especially in the village of Bony, and armoured cars and Whippets which had endeavoured to pass along the Bellicourt-Bony road had failed to make good their passage. In these circumstances an attack was planned for 30 September to clear up the canal line. It was not until 10 p.m. on the 29th that Col. Lyon received the news that his Corps Reserve tanks were to be employed in this operation. He at once got in touch with the 3rd Division of the Australian Corps, with whom the plan was arranged, and company commanders were sent to interview the infantry brigadiers. An artillery barrage was to be provided and air protection supplied. The tanks were assembled by this time in the quarry south-east of Hagricourt. The task assigned to the tanks of Maj. Morritt's company was to attack on a line on the west side of the canal towards the northern entrance of the tunnel, clearing the complicated system of trenches on the west side, assisting in the capture of Bony and extending on the final objective across the canal. The start line was roughly 1,200 yards south-west of Bony village. In theory they were to

French artillery rolls past a Mark V★ male tank which has shed a track in Domart. One of the crew discusses the situation with a group of Jocks.

A Mark V male tank, fitted with the new, wider tracks, passes a field dressing station in Domart.

cooperate with the 11th Australian Brigade, by whom guides were to be provided to lead the tanks to their starting positions; these arrangements were completed by 3 a.m. No reconnaissance at all was possible and the night was very dark.

On reaching the point on the main road east of Hagricourt, where the guides were to be waiting, no trace of them could be found. Maj. Morritt therefore moved to his start line as far as possible by road, and by 6.50 a.m. had got six tanks into position; one tank of the 16th Battalion also succeeded in completing the course and came under Maj. Morritt's command. A desultory gun fire was all that could be seen of the barrage, and no infantry appeared to be on the ground. Tanks therefore drove over the line unaccompanied, meeting with little resistance except from Bony village. There, considerable machine-gun and anti-tank rifle fire was encountered and successfully disposed of. Beyond the village a number of machine-gun nests were dealt with, and the tanks having reached their objectives returned to rally at Hagricourt at 12 noon. One officer was slightly wounded, remaining at duty, and one man was evacuated with wounds. Presumably the infantry attack could not be organized in the required time. The successful arrival of the tanks in very difficult conditions was a great personal

Mark V★ tanks working with the Australian Corps move through Roussay. The second tank, a male, has its semaphore-signalling device in operation.

triumph for Maj. Morritt; but such piratical expeditions of tanks without escort cannot be upheld as a model of tank tactics. One driver aptly summed up this exploit by saying, 'We walked down the Hindenburg Line, but luckily Hindenburg was not at home.'

On 1 October the advance was continued by the Australian Corps, assisted by other battalions of the 5th Brigade. Of the 13th Battalion eight tanks now remained serviceable at Hagricourt and these were organized into another composite company under Maj. Maurice.

On 2 October preparations were completed for an attack on the Beaurevoir Line; the last remaining defence system left to the enemy in the Hindenburg Line, with its final objectives the capture of the villages of Beaurevoir, Ponchaux and Wiancourt, and the seizure of the high ground close to Prospect Hill. Eight Mark V tanks of the 13th and six Whippets of the 3rd Battalion were allotted to the 5th Australian Brigade. Eight tanks of the 8th and 16th Battalions were given to the 7th Australian Brigade. The heavy tanks were under the command of Col. Lyon. There was ample time for the necessary liaison with the infantry to be carried out and the Australian staff were, as always, most helpful to the tanks.

Maj. Maurice's company was to start from Estrée village for the attack and had, therefore, an approach march of about 8,000 yards to make. This march presented at the very outset difficulties of an unusual kind. The night was very dark and showers of rain fell at intervals. Owing to congestion of traffic on the roads east of Hagricourt it was necessary to cross the advanced and main Hindenburg trench systems. A route had been surveyed by day, but this had been much broken by tanks in advance of the company and in places was blocked by ditched tanks of other battalions; the ground was a morass of waterlogged shell holes and broken wire. In consequence the tanks of this company were being continually ditched and pulled out by one another. The first 2,000 yards of the approach occupied 6½ hours and was very remarkable as a feat of endurance and mutual support by crews. At 2 a.m., of the eight tanks, five were ditched, one had a broken track and one was delayed by mechanical trouble. Zero was fixed for 6.05 a.m. and over 6,000 yards remained to be covered. One hour later six of the eight tanks, largely through the efforts of the tank engineer and his staff, were clear of the broken ground and it was decided to push on with these, leaving the other crews to follow when they could. North of Nauroy village the crew of the leading tank was overcome by petrol

Tanks resting in the bed of the Canal du Nord after the capture of Bourlon village on 27 September 1918. German prisoners and wounded cross in the foreground.

fumes and many of the other men were suffering from the effects. Thirty of the precious minutes remaining were devoted to reviving the crews; the column was halted, restoratives were issued out, and the men were encouraged to do breathing exercises in the fresh air. As a result all started again with new vigour and, travelling at high speed, succeeded in reaching the start line with just time to replenish petrol tanks before going into action. No. 1 Section (Capt Baker) arrived complete; of No. 2 Section (Capt Fletcher) the two tanks left behind did not arrive in time to take part in the battle; of the other battalions, three tanks reached their start line. Both sections started in the attack and caught up with their infantry before the barrage lifted. A complication at once arose at one point; information had been exact that Estrées was completely in our hands, and Australian troops of the support lines occupied the village; yet at the commencement of the advance enemy fire from concealed machine-gun posts in this village harassed the infantry on the right of the sector from the rear and for a moment held up the attack. Capt Baker at once grasped the situation and, going forward on foot through this fire, directed one of his tanks to deal with this opposition, thus enabling the infantry to press forward. The remaining tanks made good the Beaurevoir trench system and established their infantry. Sgt Rogers, detailed to engage the White House Fort, silenced this strongpoint, but before doing so received a direct hit at short range from a gun placed there; he went forward on foot and completed the task with Hotchkiss guns, after which he attached himself to the infantry and aided them to go forward.

On the right of this sector 2/Lt Smith pushed on to Wiancourt village, the final objective on his flank, from which point machine guns in the upper storeys of the houses were causing the advance to hesitate. A number of anti-tank rifles, handled by highly trained experts, were brought to bear on his tank; his driver and observer were both shot through the head and killed, two others of the crew were wounded and the tank was perforated in over twenty places. In spite of this he kept on the move, destroying many machine-gun nests, knocked out all the large rifles and silenced the enemy; the infantry were thus enabled to make their way forward into the village with no loss.

Meanwhile on the left, Capt Fletcher's two tanks, having gained their first objective and overcome all opposition, pressed on northwards towards Lamotte Farm. Here they successfully dealt with strong machine-gun resistance and then diverged. 2/Lt Childs moved north towards the Torrens Canal and cleared out the enemy entrenched along the bank. While so engaged he was bombed with stick bombs charged with phosphorus, which ignited and burnt out his engine; the crew turned out with their guns into the trench full of the enemy and killed or captured all the hostile gunners and machine guns. 2/Lt Martin, passing west of Lamotte Farm, dealt with much machine-gun opposition until his crew all

A Mark IV female tank carrying a crib, seen near Moeuvres on 27 September 1918.

became insensible with petrol fumes; he then drove his tank back to a place of safety and evacuated his unconscious crew.

The Australians here informed him that machine guns were still holding up the advance by fire from the left flank; thereupon he called for volunteers from the infantry and two Australian Lewis-gunners and one man of his crew, who had meanwhile recovered, went forward again, himself driving the tank, until all resistance had been overcome. This officer was made the subject of a very complimentary report by the Australian commander on the spot.

CHAPTER NINE

Victory

The tank actions that took place in the final weeks of the war were often scrappy affairs. The opposition might be defiant and fanatical, or collapse altogether at the slightest push. For the Tank Corps it was a matter of keeping up the pressure at all costs and that meant keeping a dwindling number of tanks and armoured cars running with a minimum of maintenance and a great deal of improvization. Although the heavy tanks were still employed, these weeks belong to the surviving Whippets and armoured cars which, alone, could maintain the speed of the pursuit. One detects a sort of nightmare quality in these final days, ending in the apparent surprise of the Armistice after that one, final burst of fire.

The Austin armoured cars had originally been built to the order of the Russian government but, following the Revolution, those still in Britain were handed over to the Tank Corps, which issued them to the 17th Battalion. They enjoyed a fine reputation from their baptism of fire, in June 1918, right through to 11 November and, as a fitting tribute, they were selected to lead the victorious British Army across the Rhine. The Austins were built on the 30 h.p. Colonial chassis with a top speed of 35 m.p.h. The twin-turret layout was much favoured by the Russians and in British service each car mounted two Hotchkiss machine guns. They carried a crew of five.

1st Battalion, 1 October 1918

On 1 October C Company rejoined the remainder of the battalion and on the 3rd A Company was merged into B and C Companies for further operations. These two composite companies moved forward to a valley on the 5th, continuing their journey the following day to the final starting point. Until the evening of the 7th all available time was spent in final adjustments and reconnaissance, and at 5.30 a.m. both companies went into that action which followed on the continued pressure of the previous week, and which completely broke down the enemy's resistance on this front. The success of the operations was complete. The infantry drove the enemy before them and, whenever necessary, tanks moved up to deal with difficult situations. Both at Hamage

Farm and Les Folies Wood sections of B Company distinguished themselves, a battery of six guns being engaged and captured by Lts Watson and Wilson at the former place. One car only was hit, the remainder rallying without casualties.

On that and the succeeding evenings a wonderful spectacle was seen in the burning of the enemy dumps and supply centres. The glow from these conflagrations lighted the sky and the surrounding country for many miles and bore witness to the precipitate retreat into which the enemy had been forced by the day's action. Destroyed bridges and crossroads marked the trail of the beaten and demoralized enemy, and the ensuing days found the battalion following in his wake at top speed. Perhaps the most gratifying part of this advance was the deliverance of villages and inhabitants which had been under the unenviable rule of the Germans since the autumn of 1914. In many cases excess of joy resulted in tears and every imaginable kind of gift was showered by the grateful villagers upon their rescuers.

The battalion finally halted in a small clearing north of Maretz and from 11–16 October the time was fully occupied in preparing for the next battle and reconnoitring the forward area. Much attention was paid to the River Selle, which was reported by civilians to be an impassable obstacle. In spite of this information two visits were made by the battalion reconnaissance officer, Capt

A squad of infantry marching past a Mark V★ male tank in a devastated village.

Bradbeer, and the B Company RO, Lt Thornbank, to the banks of the river which were in no-man's land, and eventually suitable crossings were found. The enemy's position was very strong here owing to the natural obstacle of the river and the huge railway embankment on the Le Cateau line. On the 15th all tanks in the battalion, consisting of one composite section of four tanks belonging to B Company and two composite sections, also of four tanks, belonging to C Company, moved up to their lying-up points in a small orchard north of Escaufourt, where they were camouflaged and the crews returned to rest in preparation for the action.

A start was made from here at 1 a.m. on the morning of the 17th, a previously taped route being followed. During the night gas shelling by the enemy was intense in all the valleys, and the difficulty of passing through these poisonous clouds was increased by the presence of a dense mist and the smoke from our own barrage which came down at 5.30 a.m. While this barrage was going on observation was impossible but it just lifted as B Company, which was leading, arrived at the banks of the river. Just prior to this the battalion sustained a great loss by the death of Maj. Miskin, who was killed by a shell while leading his company. All tanks succeeded

German prisoners and a wounded British soldier moving out of a gassed area as a tank waits to move forward.

in crossing the river and from there proceeded to engage the enemy who was resisting strongly along the embankment. The resistance was eventually overcome, numerous machine guns being silenced, and the infantry in the course of a strong attack dislodged the enemy from his positions. All tanks, with the exception of one which received a direct hit, returned to the rallying point and from there proceeded to the old camp at Maretz as GHQ Reserve.

A COMPANY, 12TH BATTALION, 8 OCTOBER 1918

Four tanks, *Lightning II* L9, *Lily II* L6, *Lochiel* L12 and *Lion* L16, cooperated with the 63rd Division and one tank *Lukoie III* L8 with the 57th Division in an attack on the village of Niergnes and the road to the east this morning. All tanks reached the forming-up line and had joined the infantry units to which they were allotted by Zero hour (04.30 a.m.). *Lukoie III* received a direct hit from one of our smoke shells which badly damaged the back, but the tank carried on until it became ditched over a cellar, owing to the darkness and consequent difficulty in finding the route. The tank commander (2/Lt Carmichael), while trying to find a way out, saw a body of men approaching and taking them for British troops approached them to get information. They turned out to be Germans and made him prisoner, taking him to a shell hole until our own infantry fire became intense, when he persuaded the enemy to surrender themselves to him, handing them over to the Lancashire Regiment. Owing to the position of the tank and the broken track, it was impossible to start the engine or get it out. He therefore evacuated the tank and left a guard over it.

The remaining four tanks separately reached their final objectives and saw their infantry established until the enemy counterattacked with (reported) seven tanks (Mk II type captured from the British).* These were for some time allowed to approach unmolested, being taken for British tanks, until one of them opened fire on our infantry. *Lion* then fired at it but was simultaneously knocked out by two direct hits, probably from the 6 pdr guns of other German tanks. At this time *Lily II* had nearly run out of water owing to radiator trouble, had had three Lewis guns put out of action and a direct hit on the side, and though she was still fighting the tank commander (2/Lt Martell) decided to send the crew back to take cover behind a ridge before the tank ran out of water, while he went over to an abandoned German field gun with an Artillery officer and between them served the gun effectively, knocking out two German tanks with it.

Lochiel and *Lightning II* had both been riddled with anti-tank rifle bullets and

---

*Almost certainly Mark IVs, captured after Cambrai.

A Mark IV male tank, captured by the Germans after Cambrai and fitted with their version of the six-pounder gun.

the majority of their crews wounded. 2/Lt Warcap then blew up *Lightning II* to prevent it falling into enemy hands. 2/Lt De La Mare evacuated *Lochiel* with one surviving member of the crew, Cpl Steeb, as the engine had been put entirely out of action.

In consequence of the artillery fire and anti-tank rifle fire brought to bear on the enemy tanks from captured guns and captured anti-tank rifles, the surviving crew abandoned their tanks and fled. Our infantry then consolidated their positions on the final objective.

The casualties to the company were heavy, only one tank, *Lily*, rallying, and that in damaged condition and unfit for action. Casualties to personnel amounted to almost 50 per cent; nineteen out of forty.

17TH BATTALION, 9 OCTOBER 1918

About two miles beyond Maretz they found a company of the South African Scottish, who were held up by a party of Germans in action along the north side of the main road, just beyond where the road from Busigny to Bertry cuts it. These were holding up the advance with machine guns and trench mortars. The

A pair of Austin armoured cars of 17th Battalion kick up the dust as they race foward.

armoured cars were able to run right through the machine-gun fire and engage the gunners from a flank with such effect that they fled, leaving several dead behind them, besides ten machine guns and two trench mortars.

Having dealt with that situation the cars made a dash to cross the bridge over the railway in front of Maurois. The enemy demolition party saw them coming, lit the fuse and scattered. The leading car got across safely, but the bridge blew up immediately it was across, cutting off the other car which was 50 yards in rear. So there they were, with the ruins of a bridge between them and home. However, they carried on through Maurois and then turned right towards Honnachy. Both villages were full of enemy troops which the car engaged with its fire. Near Honnachy church it ran by mistake into a byroad; at the same moment a group of Germans came out of a house to see what was happening. The car killed five of them in one doorway. This incident was described with enthusiasm to the CO when he visited the place next day, by a French woman upon whom the Germans had been billeted. Just short of Honnachy station the road from that place to Busigny is joined by another from Le Cateau. Then it turns sharply to the south and runs under the railway. Profiting by their previous

A vertical view of the road network around Maretz, where the armoured cars undertook their remarkable raid.

experience, the crew hoped to save this bridge. They came round the corner with their guns trained on the spot where they expected the demolition party to be. They were successful. One of the enemy was hit and the rest fled without lighting the fuse. In Busigny the car took on a trench-mortar battery, which was not expecting an attack from the rear, killed some of the crew and scattered the rest. It got back onto the highway by the Bertry road and picked up the other car. It had penetrated the enemy's lines, moved through a frontage of three miles over country strongly occupied by his troops, saved an important railway bridge from demolition and then returned through his lines from another direction to our Corps Headquarters with a most useful report of the situation.

In the afternoon the sections with the 7th Cavalry Brigade (Lt McKinney and 2/Lt Herd) went into action, cooperating with cavalry in an attack on Honnachy Station. Touch was gained with the cavalry at the railway bridge over the Le Cateau road. The combined attack was successful. One car was sent back to report on the situation and the three others held the road crossing and railway bridge for an hour, until the 8th Worcesters came up and took over the position, the cars thus providing a mobile strongpoint until the arrival of the infantry. The two cars in Corps Reserve, under 2/Lt Dobson, were sent about noon on a reconnaissance towards Bertry, where their counterfire against enemy machine guns considerably helped the South African Scottish in an advance against a railway cutting on the right of the road which was then held by the enemy.

The next day the battalion took up a position in Troisvilles, to the north of the main road, which was blown up in several places. The cars in Corps Reserve, accompanied by a staff officer of the Cavalry Corps, carried out a reconnaissance into Le Cateau. They found parts of the town occupied by the enemy, and the bridge in the main street badly damaged. The outskirts to the north and west were in our hands. They returned with their report. The armoured cars that night parked in Bertry, the battalion headquarters being located in a house which the previous night had been occupied by one of the German staff. We had passed the devastated area of the battle zone and had come to the region where houses were intact. The liberated population were overjoyed at the sight of British troops. Tri-colours appeared as though by magic and we realized, for the first time, what it was that the Army had really accomplished. The sight of these civilians brought it home.

Composite Tank Brigade, 4 November 1918

The tank brigade that took part in this last phase consisted of the 301st American Battalion (the only heavy tank battalion in the United States Army), the 9th, 10th and 14th tank battalions, the 6th (Whippet) Battalion and 17th (Armoured Car) Battalion, which had assisted the cavalry in chasing enemy rearguards from the Cambrai line and was much reduced in cars and personnel.

The attack on 4 November was, as it proved, the last battle of the war. Its object was to force the enemy's line from Valenciennes to Guise and on this front three British armies and one French were taking part. The 2nd Brigade eventually had tanks operating with five different Corps on a front of about 13 miles. Some of these had been suddenly diverted from their original tasks to a completely unknown area and in some cases had been just drawn from an issue park in bad mechanical condition. One section trekked 26 miles into action, or a total of 35 miles from the spot where it detrained.

These tanks were working with IV and V Corps round Ghissignies, Jolimetz and Englefontaine, while the Whippets carried on the attack on 5 November with the 2nd Guards Brigade near Buvignies. This action was completely successful and the enemy commenced a hurried withdrawal. On the Fourth Army front the Sambre-Oise Canal and the Foret de Mormal rather limited the use

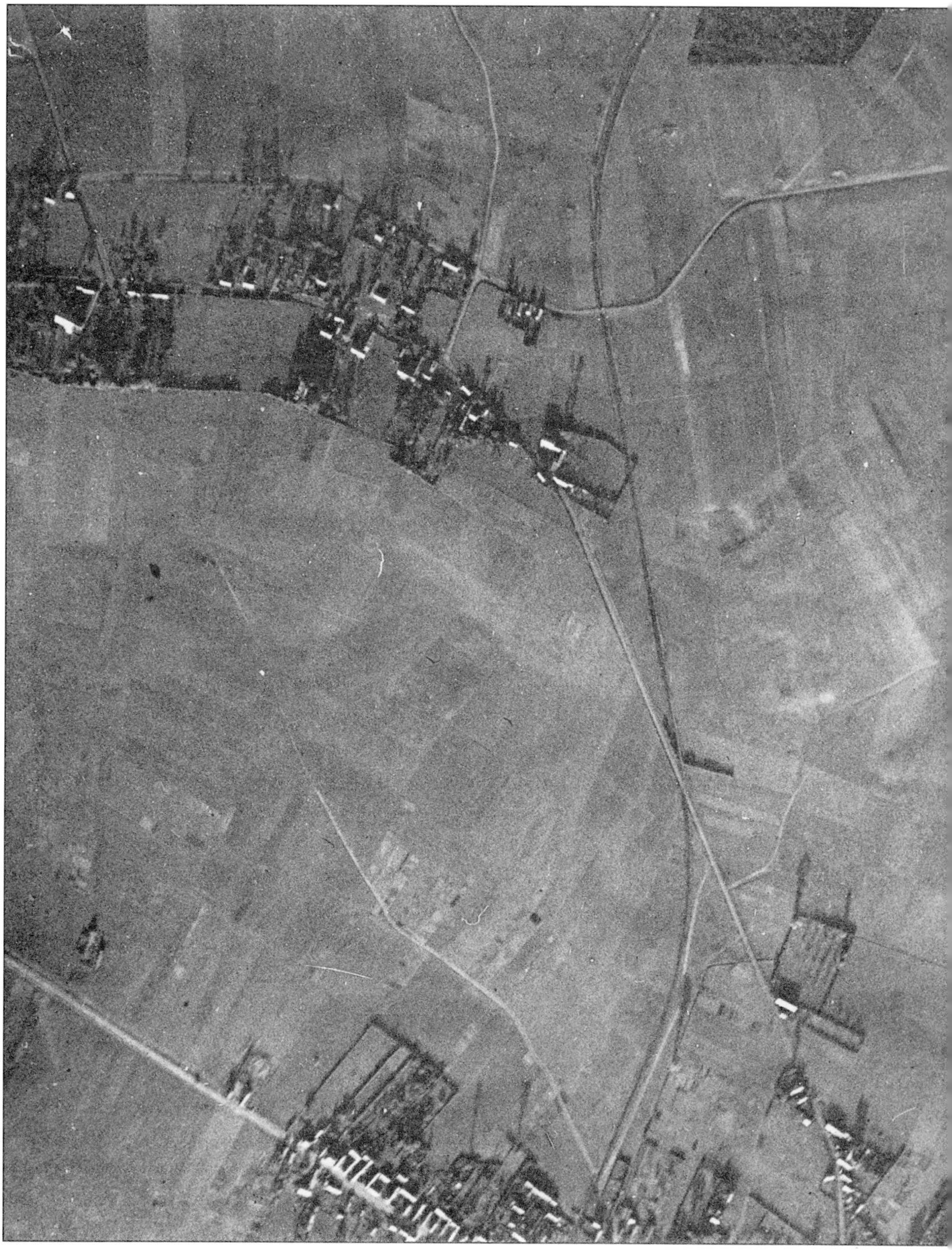

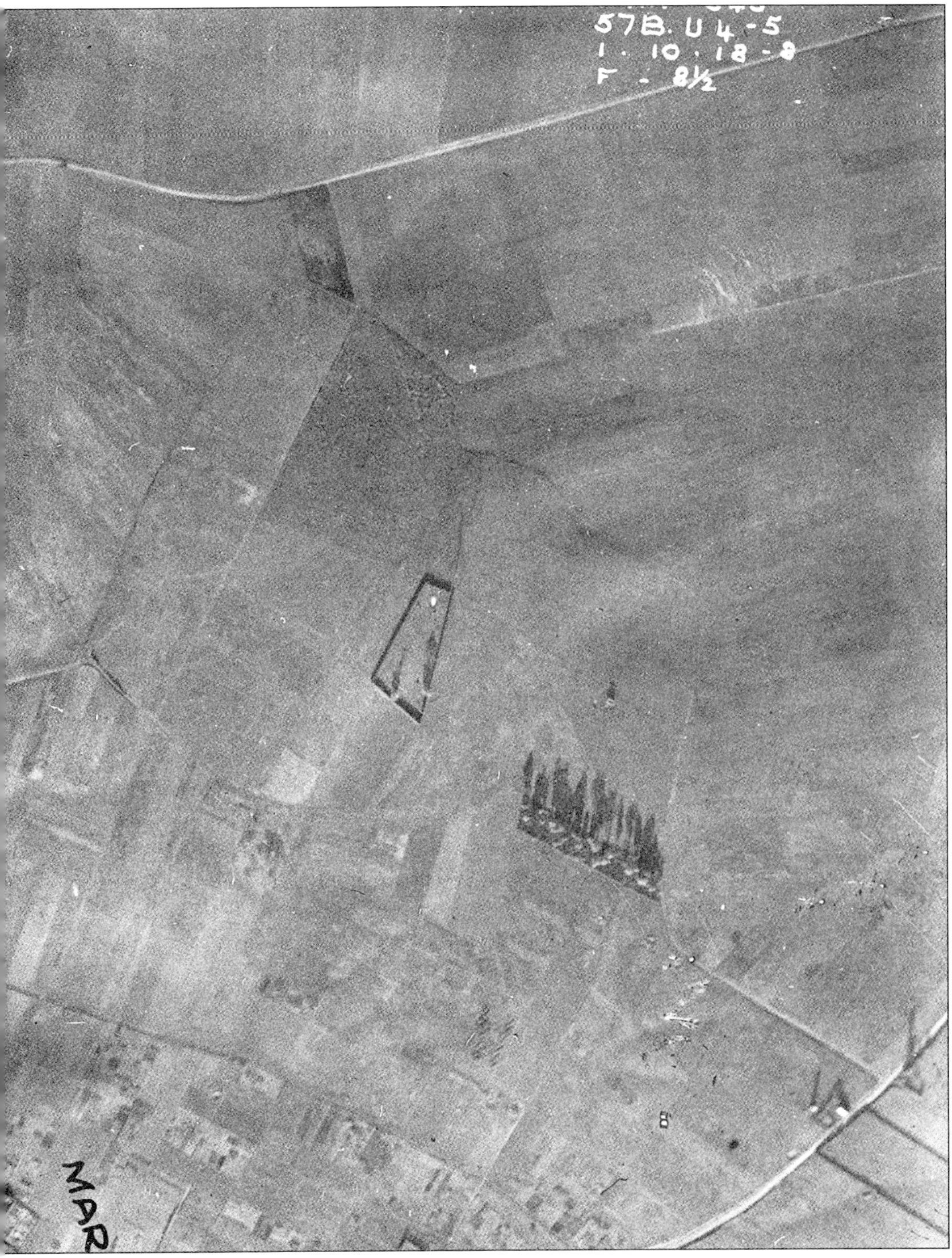
57B. U 4 - 5
1 . 10 . 18 - 8
F - 8½
MAR

A Mark V, with one track off, lies at the side of a road, while a smoke screen builds up in the valley.

of tanks, but their task was to clean up the orchard country to the edge of the forest and the rolling arable land from Happegarbes to Catillon. Twenty-one tanks from the 9th and 14th Battalions got into action with XIII Corps round Hecq, Preux and Rosimbois after a good deal of shelling on the approach march.

The attack was much hampered by mist and the blindness of the country during the early stages. One tank commander of the 14th Battalion, after his tank was disabled, took his crew on with the infantry throughout the morning and handled his Hotchkiss guns, and later a German machine gun, in a very gallant and effective way. A section commander of the 9th Battalion took in a scratch crew of Dublin Fusiliers after one of his tank crews had been gassed, and did most useful work with them. The 10th Battalion, meanwhile, who had five tanks, were working with IX Corps between Happegarbes and Catillon; one section had already helped in two minor operations on 2 and 3 November round Happegarbes and had failed to hold the captured ground, but on the 4th it was completely successful. The other section assisted in the capture of Catillon and the canal crossing.

A section of No. 2 Tank-Carrier Company, while taking bridging material down to Landrecies Lock, found the infantry held up by machine guns. The section commander decided to go on and the German machine-gunners,

VICTORY

A soldier guides a Mark IV supply tank through a ruined village. A pin-up has been attached to the front plate.

apparently thinking that fighting tanks were advancing on them, surrendered. This ended the part played by tanks in the battle. The 17th Battalion had six armoured cars in action with XIII Corps from 4 to 11 November and was specially mentioned by the Fourth Army on the 8th for its work in dispersing hostile demolition parties.

17TH BATTALION, 9 NOVEMBER 1918

On 9 November the cars were distributed as on the previous day except that one, which had been salved, completed the section with the 46th Division. At noon the commanding officer received instructions from the Fourth Army to report to the headquarters of the 66th Division. Before leaving he ordered all sections to concentrate on the Marbaix–Avesnes road. When he reached divisional headquarters he was informed of the composition and mission of Gen. Bethell's force, which was acting as Fourth Army advance guard in pursuit and operating down the main roads towards Soire le Chateau. Cars were ordered to report to his headquarters at Beugnies at 11.00 hours the following morning. All available personnel were sent to reconnoitre crossings over the Grande Helpe

A knocked-out Austin, probably mined by the state of the rear wheel. One of the turrets has also been blown off.

but every bridge was found to be destroyed. At the end of the day seven cars were fit and concentrated on the high road. Two were worked upon and would probably be fit in twelve hours.

At dawn the next day the battalion headquarters moved to Avesnes. The cars worked east down the line of the river, parallel with the advance guard of the pursuit and some 6,000 yards to the south of it, keeping in touch with Gen. Bethell's headquarters at Soire le Chateau whenever footbridges could be found across the river. They went through Semeries and Ramousies and parked for the night at Liesses. A considerable quantity of artillery, heavy guns, lorries, horse transport and three complete ammunition trains were overtaken and captured. The road craters, which appeared to have been hastily blown, were being rapidly filled in by the inhabitants, and were passable for cars. No British forces were met with, except a troop of the 20th Hussars, but touch was gained with the First French Army on our right.

On the 11th all officers reconnoitred towards Epee, Sauvage and Moustier. Battalion headquarters were situated at Liesses and were joined at 10.20 hours by a liaison officer from the 33rd French Infantry Division who were at Trelon. He

VICTORY

An Austin ready for action. The driver's cab is opened up, as is the radiator cover. Although they hardly compared with the Rolls-Royces used elsewhere during the war, these cars performed remarkably well under very difficult conditions.

gave us the first news we had of the Armistice. There was continuous firing on our left at the time, and there seemed no indication that war was to cease. A few minutes later, however, a despatch rider arrived with a wireless message from Fourth Army that hostilities were to cease at 11.00 hours. He was sent on to Gen. Bethell's headquarters with the message, together with a report of the situation of the cars at that moment. At about three minutes to eleven firing suddenly ceased along the whole front. At 11.00 hours exactly there was a final crash of gunfire, as if every gunner had simultaneously decided to have a last round at the Boche. Then all was silence. The war was over and the contrast from continuous noise to complete silence was so great as to be almost uncanny.

17TH BATTALION, 6 DECEMBER 1918

On the morning of 6 December eight cars of the 17th Battalion left Duren, where they had been resting, to escort the GOC, 2nd Cavalry Brigade into Cologne. They went by way of the road which runs through the forest, then

Symbol of Victory. A pair of Austins of 17th Battalion follow the tramlines over the Hohenzollern bridge in Cologne. Taken in December 1918, this picture shows the cars after they reached the east side of the bridge, the first Tank Corps vehicles to cross the Rhine.

across the outer military ring of concrete forts defending the city and so on to the great Roman road which runs from Aix la Chapelle up to their old bridgehead, Colonia Aggripeuse. The road runs around the old gate in the city wall, through the new market, past a statue of the 'Iron Man' and on to cross the river by an iron and stone bridge, where the Romans probably crossed it. The Hohenzollern bridge lies downstream from this. One must turn into the Cathedral Square to reach the great bridge itself, decorated with statues of all the Hohenzollern family. It was over this bridge, never before crossed by the British as conquerors, that the cars passed.

The cavalry brigade halted outside Cologne while the GOC, escorted by the armoured cars, went on to the Rathaus to arrange for the administration of the city. On 12 December Gen. Plumer, GOC Second Army, inspected the 2nd Cavalry Division. The 17th Armoured Car Battalion went past, carrying a Tank Corps flag, which it took to the limits of the perimeter to be occupied by the British Army.